English 3

Foundation Skills for 11-14 year olds

John Barber BA
Head of English,
Ward Freman School,
Buntingford

Denys Thompson MA

Charles Letts & Co Ltd
London, Edinburgh & New York

First published 1986
by Charles Letts & Co Ltd
Diary House, Borough Road, London SE1 1DW
Reprinted 1986

Illustrations: Ian David Baker, Anni Axworthy, Edward Ripley

ISBN 0 85097 667 7

Printed in Great Britain by
Charles Letts (Scotland) Ltd

By the same authors:

John Barber
Panthers' Moon
(Hutchinson)

Denys Thompson
Spelling and Punctuating
(Oxford University Press)
Change and Tradition in Rural England
(Cambridge University Press)

Acknowledgements

The authors and publishers are grateful for permission to quote from the following works:

Unit 1: 'The Baby Austin' from *Danny the Champion of the World* by Roald Dahl, published by Jonathan Cape Ltd

Units 2 and 18: 'The Dog that Bit People' and 'The Night the Bed Fell' from *Vintage Thurber* by James Thurber, published by Hamish Hamilton Ltd © Hamish Hamilton 1963

Unit 3: 'Salvatore' from *Collected Short Stories* Volume IV by W. Somerset Maugham, reproduced by permission of the Executors of the Estate of W. Somerset Maugham and William Heinemann Ltd

Unit 4: *No Place Like* by Gene Kemp, reprinted by permission of Faber and Faber Ltd

Unit 5: *Vaulting Ambition* by Simon Barnes from the *Mail on Sunday YOU* magazine. *The Trampoline* by John Pudney, reproduced by permission of David Higham Associates Limited

Unit 6: *The Lantern Bearers* by Rosemary Sutcliff (1959) by permission of Oxford University Press

Unit 8: *Apostate* by Forrest Reid, reproduced by permission of the author's literary executor Stephen Gilbert

Unit 9: *East End at Your Feet* by Farrukh Dhondy, published by Macmillan, London and Basingstoke

Unit 10: 'His First Flight' from *The Short Stories of Liam O'Flaherty*, reproduced by permission of the Estate of Liam O'Flaherty and Jonathan Cape Ltd

Unit 11: *A Foreign Affair* by John Rowe Townsend, copyright © 1982 by John Rowe Townsend, published by Kestrel Books, 1982

Unit 12: 'Thanks' from *The Book of Fub* by Michael Frayn © Michael Frayn 1963, reproduced by permission of Elaine Green Ltd, Literary Agency

Unit 13: *Last to Go* by Harold Pinter, published by Methuen London

Unit 14: *The Living Planet* by David Attenborough, published by Collins. *Volcano*: Ordeal by Fire in Iceland's Westman Islands by May and Hallberg Hallmundsson, translated by Arni Gunnarsson, published in 1973 by Iceland Review

Unit 15: 'Boy' from *The Stories of Frank Sargeson*, published by Penguin Books (N Z) Ltd, 1982

Unit 16: *Julie of the Wolves* by Jean C. George, published by Harper & Row, reprinted by permission of Curtis Brown, Ltd, New York

Unit 17: *The Golden Grindstone* by Angus Graham, reprinted by permission of A D Peters & Co Ltd. *Old Wolf* by James Taylor. We regret that it has proved impossible to trace the copyright holder of this poem.

Unit 19: *Faith and Henry* by Julia Jones, reproduced by permission of the author and Jill Foster Ltd

Unit 20: *A Precocious Autobiography* by Yevgeny Yevtushenko, published by Collins Harvill. The extract from *Danny Blanchflower's Soccer Book*, published by Muller, Blond & White Ltd

Unit 23: *Robot Revolt* by Nicholas Fisk, published by Pelham Books Ltd

Units 25 and 26: *The Village by the Sea* by Anita Desai, copyright © Anita Desai, 1982, reprinted by permission of William Heinemann Limited

Unit 27: *Encounters with Animals* by Gerald Durrell, published by Grafton Books, a Division of the Collins Publishing Group

Unit 28: *Empty World* by John Christopher, reproduced by permission of Sam Youd

Unit 29: *The Fortunate Few* by Tim Kennemore, reprinted by permission of Faber and Faber Ltd

Unit 30: *Under Goliath* by Peter Carter (1977) by permission of Oxford University Press

Unit 31: *Mrs Frisby and the Rats of NIMH* by Robert C. O'Brien, published by Victor Gollancz Ltd

Unit 32: 'A Many Splendoured Thing' from *England our England* by Keith Waterhouse and Willis Hall, reproduced by permission of Harvey Unna & Stephen Durbridge Ltd

Unit 33: *Yet Being Someone Other* by Laurens van der Post, published by The Hogarth Press

Unit 34: *Twenty Years A-Growing* by Maurice O'Sullivan, reproduced by permission of the author's estate and Chatto & Windus

Unit 37: *Around the World on Pocket Money* by Peter Waymark from *The Times* (11.2.1984). *Stamp Collection* by Tony Lucas, published by Outposts Poetry Quarterly, reproduced by permission of the author

Unit 38: *Song of the Wagon Driver* by B. S. Johnson, © the Estate of B. S. Johnson 1986; first published by Constable and Co Ltd, 1964

Unit 39: 'The Breadwinner' from *To Tea on Sunday* by Leslie Halward, published by E. Arnold, reproduced by permission of David Higham Associates Limited

Unit 40: Article by Arthur Reed from a series entitled 'On This Day' *The Times* (22.1.1985).

Unit 41: *Mr Brunswick and I* by Charles Stephens, first printed in *Imagine*, reproduced by permission of The National Association for the Teaching of English (NATE Publications)

Unit 45: *Tiger Eyes* by Judy Blume, copyright © Judy Blume 1981, reprinted by permission of William Heinemann Limited

Unit 46: *Cider with Rosie* by Laurie Lee, published by The Hogarth Press

Unit 47: 'Ha'penny' from *Debbie Go Home* by Alan Paton, published by Jonathan Cape Ltd

Unit 48: *A Fortunate Man* by John Berger, published by Allen Lane The Penguin Press, 1967, reproduced by kind permission of Curtis Brown

Unit 49: *Break in the Sun* by Bernard Ashley (1980) by permission of Oxford University Press

Unit 50: 'Daily London Recipe' and 'The Creation of Man's Best Friend' both from *Up to Date* by Steve Turner, reprinted by permission of Hodder and Stoughton Limited. *Grandmother's House* by Berenice Moore, published by Outposts Poetry Quarterly, reproduced by permission of the author, *Statue of Isaac Newton, Grantham,* by David Holliday published by Outposts Poetry Quarterly, reproduced by permission of the author. We regret that it has proved impossible to trace the copyright holders of the poem *Leopard* and also the poem *Getting Home* by Neil Hoggan

We are grateful to the following organizations and individuals for permitting us to reproduce photographs for which they hold the copyright:

Aerofilms: p 98; J. Allan Cash Ltd: p 36; Ian Beames/Ardea London: p 65; Liz and Tony Bomford/Ardea London: p 73; John Marchington/Ardea London: p 30; Associated Press Ltd: pp 50, 51, 57; BBC Hulton Picture Library: p 108; Barnaby's Picture Library: pp 89, 97; Tony Boxall FRPS/Barnaby's Picture Library: p 53; Richard Chowen/Barnaby's Picture Library: p 94; Gerald Clyde/Barnaby's Picture Library: p 17; Richard Gee/Barnaby's Picture Library: p 45; Brian Robson/Barnaby's Picture Library: p 96; Peter Trievnor/Barnaby's Picture Library: p 36; British Aircraft Corporation Ltd: pp 91, 92; Camera Press: pp 103, 105; Richard Harrington/Camera Press: p 43; Mary Evans Picture Library: p 81; Pam Isherwood/Format: pp 71, 86; Jenny Mathews/Format: pp 58-9, 85; Sally and Richard Greenhill: p 48; Robert Harding Picture Library: pp 38, 39; The Trustees of the Imperial War Museum, London: p 104; Japan Information Centre: p 77; Barry Lewis/Network: p 109; London Weekend Television: p 48; MGM and the National Film Archive, London: p 100; The Mansell Collection: pp 74, 83, 102; Flip Schulke/Planet Earth Pictures: Seaphot Ltd: p 79; Popperfoto: pp 20, 24, 51, 62, 67, 69, 85; The Royal Mint: p 88; Trustees of the Science Museum, London: p 114; Ronald Sheridan's Photo-Library: pp 22-3; p 101: still from the film *Romeo and Juliet* by courtesy of The Rank Organisation plc and the National Film Archive, London.

Preface

For parents in particular

In the Preface to Volumes 1 and 2 we stressed the need for parental support and encouragement. We suggested active help in talking, listening, reading and writing; for success in English depends on plenty of practice in these four modes.

Few would, or could, deny that we live in a bewildering world. Being able to talk coolly, listen to the thoughts and opinions of others, and reach conclusions (always being ready to modify them), is crucial. To this end, we have introduced several units on subjects about which young teenagers are beginning to hold strong opinions. Though young people are outwardly sophisticated – society tends to encourage them to grow up very quickly – they need to increase their competence in their mother tongue, and we hope that this book will provide substantial material. Having books around the home, and with parents reading them, can have an important influence. A parent watching videos every evening who nags a son or daughter to go and read 'because it's good for you' is not providing the necessary encouragement and example.

Sooner or later, rightly or wrongly, the question of examinations presents itself. These volumes provide a grounding in the skills necessary for achieving success, though, as we have implied above, English goes much beyond examinations. In the units we have concentrated on encouraging the reader to have something to say, for there is no point in having skills without ideas. In the three volumes, we have systematically covered many points of style, spelling and punctuation. We believe strongly in a 'drip-feed' approach; frequent reminders, reasons and explanations to keep accuracy in the reader's mind, but without making accuracy the principal aim.

Following on from the three volumes in the Foundation Skills Series is *Revise English*, a volume specifically designed for candidates in public examinations at 16+.

In preparing the three volumes, we have taken into account the following: *A Language for Life* (HMSO 1975), the tasks tested by the *Assessment of Performance* unit set up in 1975, *Aspects of Secondary Education in England* (HMSO 1979), and *English from Five to Sixteen* (HMSO 1984).

We wish to thank Michael Wenham for his critical and helpful comments in the preparation of these volumes.

Contents

Introduction

When you've been to a party that you've specially enjoyed, you probably want to talk about it. It's natural to talk; it helps us to keep alive something of our enjoyment. The good bits, in particular, become fixed in our memories. Almost certainly you won't have realized that you were 'doing English'. *Talking* is important, and developed a long, long, time before writing. It is one of the four areas of English we will be encouraging in this book.

Listening, another of the four areas, goes hand-in-hand with talking. After all, if you talk to someone you expect him to listen to you, and it's only right for you to listen when someone else does the talking. Apart from conversation, you need to listen carefully to instructions and in lessons.

Reading and *writing* complete our four areas of English. We hope that you will enjoy the pieces we have chosen and be tempted to read as many as you can of the books we recommend. Getting 'hooked on books' will give you hours and hours of pleasure, and gradually filling your book shelves with books is like increasing your number of friends. Books make good friends – they can't answer back!

Melvyn Bragg, who is a novelist apart from being a television presenter and producer, has said how exciting he finds *writing*. He remembers vividly writing his first short story. He hadn't sat down with the intention of writing a story, but he found himself starting a story and he was completely taken up by it. In fact, he doesn't even know how long he spent writing because he found it so absorbing. This is a case of getting 'hooked on writing'. And what a cheap and satisfying hobby writing can be; all you need is some paper and a pen or pencil.There can't be many cheaper hobbies.

Melvyn Bragg – writer and broadcaster

Why bother with English? First, as we hope you have already gathered, we think it's exciting and we would like you to do so too. Secondly, the better you are at English, the better you will become at most of your other subjects, and that's a pretty good reason, isn't it? Thirdly, and this stems from the last reason, such importance is attached to how good you are at English, not just while you are at school, but after you have left. The firmer you build the foundations now, the easier will the future become.

English is a subject that all schools take seriously, but unfortunately the number of lessons has to be limited. This book will give you that extra practice that will help you improve and will explain the skills (spelling, punctuation, style, and so on) you may be unsure about.

What each unit contains

We begin each unit with a piece from a short story, novel, article, play, or poem. Sometimes we have written an introductory sentence or two to explain or to help to set the scene. We offer a wide range of topics (what happened when Pete Williams failed his exams; how Faith and Henry respond differently to cheese; volcanoes; how a Russian poet nearly became a professional footballer; what it is like being stuck in a maze), and we hope you will enjoy reading them. There are bound to be some that appeal more than others, of course.

We have usually written a

Comment

for you to read after the main piece. You will find more information about the book or the author, and we have tried to draw your attention to aspects we consider important. In some cases, having read the Comment, you will probably find it worthwhile to re-read the piece to which it applies.

Most of your time will be spent on the

Activities

which we have tried to make as varied and interesting for you as possible. We suggest listening, talking, reading and writing activities. But please don't feel that you have to work through *every* activity. You will be able to write stories and poems, make lists and tables, question friends and relations, record conversations, research in libraries and museums, curl up in a corner with a book. In some of the activities we ask you questions without indicating what we expect you to do with your answers. For these activities, think carefully about the question; it is obvious that we all have differing experiences, so our aim has been to try to jog *your* particular memory. Please think of possible ways of treating an activity. Part of the art of succeeding in English is to look for possibilities, there being many more than you probably realize.

Each unit apart from two finishes with

Nuts and Bolts

which gives you hints, skills and terms you will find useful in improving the technical accuracy of your English. The emphasis, as our name for the section suggests, is on practical English.

There is no answer section in this book because the activities can have many possible responses. And the few questions that have a definite answer have sufficient clues for you to know if you are right.

What you need

Where do you write your notes and stories and poems? We recommend that you have the following, though it is really a matter of personal choice:

(a) a *notebook*

- ► for writing a first draft (or rough copy) which you will work on and improve before writing a fair copy,
- ► for jotting down notes from encyclopedias in libraries,
- ► for noting questions you want to ask, etc.

In short, a multi-purpose notebook that can be taken around conveniently

(b) a *folder* or *binder,* together with a pad of paper (both lined and plain)

► for your finished activities

(c) a *dictionary* is an essential guide to have and *use* while working through the book

(d) If you come across any poems or short extracts in the course of your reading that you particularly enjoy, write them out neatly in a *stiff-covered exercise book.*

(e) We suggest that, if you have become enthusiastic about a topic, you might like to have a separate *folder* just for that topic and carry out many more activities than we have given. (A project on volcanoes, for example.)

(f) A *cassette recorder* would be useful for some activities, but you can make good use of the book without one.

Handwriting

Good, legible handwriting is an asset both in school and in later life. If your handwriting is slovenly and difficult to read, now is the time to do something about it. There are various styles, but they all have several points in common:

► they are legible,

► the letters are even (a e o r, for example, are all the same height),

► if the letters slant at all at least they slant the same way. This is especially important with those letters that project below the line.

Presentation

Apart from taking care with handwriting, you should try to make the overall appearance of a page attractive. Leave a clear margin all round, training your eye to avoid a line ending in a jumbled group of letters crammed together.

How to use the table (pages 10-11)

On the left-hand side of the table you will see the titles of the units, while across the top of the pages you will see two sections: the first refers to listening and talking, reading and writing *Activities*; and the second indicates topics covered in *Nuts and bolts*. You can use the table as a quick reference guide. Greater detail is given in the Index on pages 119–120.

ACTIVITIES

We have numbered the activities here and in the index for ease of reference. Had we done so in the units you might have felt they had to be answered in sequence and this is not the case.

		Thinking and noting	Imaginative & descriptive writing	Personal experience	Lists/tables/charts	Diaries	Letters	Poetry	Script/dialogue	Conversation/oral work	Reports and summaries	News items and headlines	Research	Dictionary work	Reading	Miscellaneous
1	My heart was thumping away	1	2	2	3										4	
2	Muggs		5				3	2	1				4	4		
3	Salvatore	1	2, 5		3											4
4	A strong pong of grilled grill		1, 3							2	4				5	
5	Vaulting ambition	1	4	3, 5		2									6	
6	Escape from slavery	2	1						3				4, 5		6, 7	
7	Like words, hate words, calm words	2	3		5							4		2		1
8	The adventure was over	2, 5	4	1		3				7					6	
9	Indian girl and English boy	1, 3, 4							5	2			7		6	
10	His first flight		2	1				5					3, 4	6		
11	More heat than light	1	3	3		2	5				4					
12	Thank you		1, 5				2, 3			4						
13	Last to go		3						1	2					4	
14	The furnaces of the Earth				2					3	3	1	6, 8	4, 5		7
15	The cat sat on the mat		1	1											2	
16	A father no more	1, 2	6		3								4		5	
17	Hunted by wolves	1	3, 4							4	2	2	3		5	
18	The night the bed fell		1	2		4				5				6	3	
19	Faith and Henry			5	2			5	1		3		4			
20	Kicking a ball about	1, 4	3		1		4					2			5	
21	Personal letters						1								3	2
22	Business letters						1, 2									3
23	The robots revolt	1	4		2							3			5	
24	It pays to advertise	1, 4, 5														1, 2, 3
25	Lila	1, 4			2		3								5	
26	Hari fends for himself	4, 5	1	1				2	3							
27	In a hole full of snakes	2, 4	1	1									5		3	
28	Empty world	3, 4	1, 2													
29	Shepherds Bushwhackers	4, 6					2		5	4	1	3				
30	Thinking about Riley	3	4						2				3		5	1
31	Rat civilization	2									1	3	5		4	
32	Girl meets boy	4			3		1		5				2	4		
33	Jiu-jitsu	2	4	4, 5		2					1		6	3		1
34	The whale	1											2, 3		4, 5	
35	Absentmindedness in the choir	1	3				4					2	5, 6		6	
36	No place to go	1							2	1	4		6	6	3, 5	
37	Around the world on pocket money		3	3			1				2				4	
38	Ballads							1					3		2	
39	The breadwinner		1, 2, 3						4	5					6	
40	The supersonic era begins	1, 3										2	4, 5			
41	Mr Brunswick and I	1, 3					4				2	5				
42	Happy evenings		2	1						5					3, 4	
43	Amazed	1, 6	3										2			4, 5
44	Out, you baggage!	3					4			2						1, 2
45	Something is wrong	1, 2		3											4	
46	Uncle Charles	1, 7	2									3	4	5, 6		
47	Ha'penny	2	4	4		1					3				5	
48	Emergency!	1, 2, 3			5		4						1			
49	A huge emptiness	3	1					4	2						5	
50	That's life!	–see the third and fourth paragraphs of the unit–														

NUTS AND BOLTS

	The right word	Slang	Idioms	Like words, etc	Style	Metaphors and similes	Order	Italics	Paragraphs	Parts of speech	Clauses and phrases	Commas	Full-stops	Colons and semi-colons	Dashes, etc	Hyphens	Quotations	Apostrophes	Prefixes	-er, -or	Soft c and g	Plurals	Families	Spelling revision	Dictionary
							●			●														●	
									●																
					●				●	●													●		
		●			●												●							●	
						●								●			●							●	
	●							●		●														●	
		●							●																●
	●								●														●		
																		●							
			●													●								●	
			●						●															●	
					●					●						●									
					●			●					●					●							
	●					●																●			
					●																	●		●	
	●							●		●					●								●	●	
					●					●													●		
					●			●																●	
	●				●																			●	
					●	●								●	●									●	
							●		●			●								●				●	●
	●				●																				
					●		●																		
					●				●														●	●	
					●					●					●										
																			●						
																			●				●		
											●								●					●	
							●				●														●
												●												●	
												●		●	●			●							
								●								●									●
					●				●																
					●																				
							●		●													●			
	●								●																
										●															
					●		●		●	●											●				
	●				●	●				●															
				●						●											●				
				●	●																				
										●														●	
	●																								
								●	●																
									●																
							●										●							●	
					●				●															●	
			●		●	●	●			●															

Unit 1

My heart was thumping away

Danny, whose father runs a garage, is anxiously awaiting his father's return from a poaching trip:

I stood on a chair and lit the oil-lamp in the ceiling. I had some weekend homework to do and this was as good a time as any to do it. I laid my books out on the table and sat down. But I found it impossible to keep my mind on my work.

I closed my books and decided to go to bed instead. I undressed, put on my pyjamas and climbed into my bunk. I left the lamp burning. Soon I fell asleep.

When I opened my eyes again, the oil-lamp was still glowing and the clock on the wall said ten minutes past two.

Ten minutes past two!

I jumped out of my bunk and looked into the bunk above mine. It was empty.

He had promised he would be home by ten-thirty at the latest, and he never broke promises.

He was nearly four hours overdue!

It took me two seconds to decide what I should do.

Very quickly I stripped off my pyjamas and put on my shirt and my jeans. How long would it take me to get to the wood? An hour and a half. Less if I ran most of the way, but not much less.

Thank heavens I knew the way.

But it was going to be a long hard slog. I must try to keep a good steady pace and not run myself to a standstill in the first mile.

At that point a wild and marvellous idea came to me. Why shouldn't I go in the old Austin? I really did know how to drive. My father had always allowed me to move the cars around when they came in for repair. He let me drive them into the workshop and back them out again afterwards. I loved doing it. And I would get there much quicker if I went by car. I had never driven on the road, but I would surely not meet any other cars at this time of night. I would go very slowly.

I went back to the workshop and switched on the light. I got into the driver's seat and turned the ignition key. The motor coughed once, then started.

I felt for the clutch pedal with my toe. I was just able to reach it, but I had to point my toe if I wanted to press it all the way down. I pressed it down. Then I slipped the gear-lever into reverse. Slowly I backed the car out of the workshop.

I left her ticking over and went back to switch off the workshop light. I got back into the car. The sidelights were so dim I hardly knew they were there. I switched on the headlamps. That was better. I put the headlamps on full. They didn't give any more light than a couple of good torches.

I pressed down the clutch pedal again and pushed the gear-lever into first. This was it. My heart was thumping away so fiercely I could hear it in my throat. Ten yards away lay the main road. I released the clutch very slowly. At the same time, I pressed down just a fraction of an inch on the accelerator with my right toe, and stealthily, oh most wonderfully, the little car began to lean forward and steal into motion. I pressed a shade harder on the accelerator. We crept out on to the dark deserted road.

I will not pretend I wasn't petrified. I was. But mixed in with the awful fear was a glorious feeling of excitement. Most of the really exciting things we do in our lives scare us to death. They wouldn't be exciting if they didn't. I sat very stiff and upright in my seat, gripping the steering-wheel tight with both hands. My eyes were about level with the top of the steering wheel.

The road seemed awfully narrow in the dark. At any moment something with blazing headlamps might come roaring towards me at sixty miles an hour. Was I too much in the middle of the road? Yes, I was. But I didn't want to pull in closer for fear of hitting the bank and busting the front axle, then all would be lost.

The motor was beginning to rattle and shake. I was still in first gear. It was vital to change up into second otherwise the engine would get too hot. I knew how the change was done but I had never actually tried doing it.

I eased my foot off the accelerator. I pressed the clutch down and held it there. I found the gear-lever and pulled it straight back, from first into second. I released the clutch and pressed on the accelerator. The little car leaped forward as though it had been stung. We were in second gear.

What speed were we doing? I glanced at the speedometer. It said fifteen miles an hour. Good. That was quite fast enough. I would stay in second gear.

I kept going. Once a fox flashed out of the hedge in front of me and ran across the road with his long bushy tail streaming out behind him. I saw him clearly in the glow of my headlamps. His fur was red-brown and he had a white muzzle. It was a thrilling sight. I began to worry about the motor. I knew very well it would be certain to overheat if I drove for long in either first or second gear. I was in second. I must now change up into third. I took a deep breath and grasped the gear-lever again. Foot off the accelerator. Clutch in. Gear lever up and across and up again. Clutch out. I had done it! I pressed down on the accelerator. The speedometer crept up to thirty. I gripped the wheel very tight with both hands and stayed in the middle of the road. At this rate I would soon be there.

Suddenly, far ahead of me I saw a splash of yellow light. I watched it, trembling. Very quickly the light got brighter and brighter, and nearer and nearer, and in a few seconds it took shape and became the long white beam of headlamps from a car rushing towards me.

The little engine roared. The speedometer needle went from thirty to thirty-five and then to forty. But the other car was closing fast. Its headlamps were like two dazzling white eyes. They grew bigger and bigger and suddenly the whole road in front of me was lit up as clear as daylight, and *swish*! the thing went past me like a bullet. It was so close I felt the wind of it through my open window. And in that tiny fraction of a second when the two of us were alongside one another, I caught a glimpse of its white-painted body and I knew it was the police.

I didn't dare look round to see if they were stopping and coming back after me. I was certain they would stop. Any policeman in the world would stop if he suddenly passed a small boy in a tiny car chugging along a lonely road at half-past two in the morning.

Danny the Champion of the World:
Roald Dahl

Comment

Danny seems a resourceful and daring character; he thinks and acts quickly in his anxiety to find out what has happened to his father. He feels both frightened and excited at the same time.

The old car becomes a companion, Danny referring to the car and himself as 'we': '*We* crept out . . .' and '*We* were in second gear . . .'.

Activities

– Have you ever felt the mixture of fear and excitement that Danny felt? Perhaps you have when you've been learning an outdoor sport like ski-ing or mountaineering? Do you agree with the statement, 'Most of the really exciting things we do in our lives scare us to death. They wouldn't be exciting if they didn't'? Make a note of your thoughts.
– 'Quick decision.' Write a story, perhaps based on your own experience, with this title.
– Pick out the various actions necessary for starting and driving a car. Either from your own knowledge or by watching a driver carefully, check to see how accurately the author has described Danny's actions. Write detailed instructions as a flow chart, like this:

Insert ignition key
↓
Gear lever in neutral
↓
Turn ignition key
↓
Depress clutch
and so on.

– Did the police stop as soon as they had passed Danny? What had happened to Danny's father? Read Roald Dahl's book to find out.

Nuts and Bolts

Find the paragraph 'I felt for the clutch', and look at the last sentence. The normal **order** would be to place 'slowly' after 'the car'. Why is 'slowly' at the beginning? Find another example of this changed order in the next paragraph but one.

In the paragraph 'I pressed down the clutch', find four **adverbs**, all ending in **ly**. Think of the four **adjectives** on which they are based; and note carefully what happens when **ly** is added.

'Always' is made up of 'all' and 'ways'. Think of two more 'al-' words. Remember that we do not join 'all' and 'right'.

Unit 2

Muggs

The Thurbers had an Airedale dog of this name. 'Mother used to send a box of candy every Christmas to the people the Airedale bit. The list finally contained forty or more names.' Our extract starts with one of Thurber's arguments with Muggs who had bitten him. So he picked the animal up by the tail and flung him into the kitchen:

But I forgot about the backstairs. Muggs went up the backstairs and down the frontstairs and had me cornered in the living room. I managed to get up onto the mantelpiece, but it gave way and came down with a tremendous crash throwing a large marble clock, several vases and myself heavily to the floor. Muggs was so alarmed by the racket that when I picked myself up he had disappeared. We couldn't find him anywhere, although we whistled and shouted, until old Mrs Detweiler called after dinner that night. Muggs had bitten her once, in the leg, and she came into the living room only after we assured her that Muggs had run away. She had just seated herself when, with a great growling and scratching of claws, Muggs emerged from under a sofa where he had been quietly hiding all the time, and bit her again. Mother examined the bite and put arnica on it and told Mrs Detweiler that it was only a bruise. 'He just bumped you,' she said. But Mrs Detweiler left the house in a nasty state of mind.

Lots of people reported our Airedale to the police but my father held a municipal office at the time and was on friendly terms with the police. Even so, the cops had been out a couple of times – once when Muggs bit Mrs Rufus Sturtevant and again when he bit Lieutenant-Governor Malloy – but mother told them that it hadn't been Muggs' fault but the fault of the people who were bitten. 'When he starts for them, they scream,' she explained, 'and that excites him.' The cops suggested that it might be a good idea to tie the dog up, but mother said that it mortified him to be tied up and that he wouldn't eat when he was tied up.

Muggs at his meals was an unusual sight. Because of the fact that if you reached toward the floor he would bite you, we usually put his food plate on top of an old kitchen table with a bench alongside the table. Muggs would stand on the bench and eat. I remember that my mother's brother Uncle Horatio, who boasted that he was the third man up Missionary Ridge, was splutteringly indignant when he found out that we fed the dog on a table because we were afraid to put his plate on the floor. He said he wasn't afraid of any dog that ever lived and that he would put the dog's plate on the floor if we would give it him. Roy said that if Uncle Horatio had fed Muggs on the ground just before the battle he would have been the first man up Missionary Ridge. Uncle Horatio was furious. 'Bring him in! Bring him in!' he shouted. 'I'll feed the ---- on the floor!' Roy was all for giving him a chance, but my father wouldn't hear of it. He said that Muggs had already been fed. 'I'll feed him again!' bawled Uncle Horatio. We had quite a time quieting him.

In his last year Muggs used to spend practically all of his time outdoors. He didn't like to stay in the house for some reason or other – perhaps it held too many unpleasant memories for him. Anyway, it was hard to get him to come in and as a result the garbage man, the iceman and the laundryman wouldn't come near the house. We had to haul the garbage down to the corner, take the laundry out and bring it back, and meet the iceman a block from home. After this had gone on for some time we hit on an ingenious arrangement for getting the dog in the house so that we could lock him up while the gas meter was read. Muggs was afraid of only one thing, an electrical storm. Thunder and lightning frightened him out of his senses. (I think he thought a storm had broken the day the mantelpiece fell.) He would rush into the house and hide under a bed or in a clothes closet. So we fixed up a thunder machine out of a long narrow piece of sheet iron with a wooden handle on one end. Mother would shake this vigorously when she wanted to get Muggs into the house. It made an excellent imitation of thunder, but I suppose it was the most roundabout system for running a household that was ever devised. It took a lot out of mother.

A few months before Muggs died, he got to 'seeing things.' He would rise slowly from the floor, growling low, and stalk stiff-legged and menacing toward nothing at all. Sometimes the Thing would be just a little to right or left of a visitor. Once a Fuller Brush salesman got hysterics. Muggs came wandering into the room like Hamlet following his father's ghost. His eyes were fixed on a spot just to the left of the Fuller Brush man, who stood it until Muggs was about three slow, creeping paces from him. Then he shouted. Muggs wavered on past him into the hallway grumbling to himself, but the Fuller man went on shouting. I think mother had to throw a pan of cold water on him before he stopped. That was the way she used to stop us boys when we got into fights.

Muggs died quite suddenly one night. Mother wanted to bury him in the family lot under a marble stone with some such inscription as 'Flights of angels sing thee to thy rest' but we persuaded her that it was against the law. In the end we just put up a smooth board above his grave along a lonely road. On the board I wrote with an indelible pencil 'Cave Canem'. Mother was quite pleased with the simple classic dignity of the old Latin epitaph.

The Thurber Carnival:
James Thurber

Comment

We have included several pieces by James Thurber in this series because we enjoy his humour and zest for life – though we doubt whether Mrs Detweiler was of the same opinion. There seems never to have been a boring moment in the Thurber household.

Activities

– Imagine a conversation between Mrs Detweiler and Uncle Horatio about Muggs. What might they have said to each other? Write the dialogue in script form.
– Write a short poem about Muggs, trying particularly to express something of the dog's personality.
– Imagine you are one of the 'forty or more' bitten by Muggs. Write a letter to Mrs Thurber thanking her for the box of candy, but politely saying that you would rather have not been bitten in the first place.
– Look up the meaning of 'epitaph' in a dictionary. What does the Latin *Cave Canem* mean?
– Read this short extract from *Hotel du Lac* by Anita Brookner (the novel won the 1984 Booker McConnell prize) and rewrite it as if you were James Thurber witnessing the incident. Try to capture his humour.

At the foot of the stairs crouched a very small dog, quivering with anxiety, its eyes covered by its hair. When no one came to see what was wrong, it started up again at full volume, but experimentally, like a baby. A prolonged keening, as if it were undergoing unimaginable torture, brought cries of 'Kiki! Kiki! Naughty dog!', and a tall woman, of extraordinary slenderness, and with the narrow nodding head of a grebe, rushed out of the bar, collapsed at the foot of the stairs, gathered the dog into her arms, covered it with kisses, and again, with the same boneless uncoiling movement, pressed the dog to her face like a cushion, and returned to the bar. A puddle on the last step brought a momentary closing of the eyes and a quick snap of the fingers from the manager. As a boy in a white jacket wielded a cloth, impassively, as if this happened fairly often, the manager indicated to Edith Hope his distress that this incident should mar her arrival, and at the same time expressed dissociation from the misdemeanours of animals and, more important, from those unwise enough to harbour them.

Nuts and Bolts

From an early age, children enjoy jig-saw puzzles; there is something very satisfying about fitting the pieces together. In this book we shall be setting some examples of a word puzzle: the sorting out of sentences (the pieces) of a jumbled paragraph. We shall ask you to do your own jumbling, and then after a gap remind you to sort the sentences out. Here are the first four sentences of *Muggs* in random order, to show you what we mean:
– Muggs was so alarmed by the racket that when I picked myself up he had disappeared.
– I managed to get up onto the mantelpiece, but it gave way and came down with a tremendous crash throwing a large marble clock, several vases and myself heavily to the floor.
– Muggs went up the backstairs and down the frontstairs and had me cornered in the living room.
– But I forgot about the backstairs.
Cover the opposite page with a piece of paper and see if you can put these sentences in the right order.

Unit 3

Salvatore

I wonder if I can do it.

I knew Salvatore first when he was a boy of fifteen with a pleasant face, a laughing mouth, and carefree eyes. He was in and out of the sea all the time, swimming. Scrambling up the jagged rocks on his hard feet, for except on Sundays he never wore shoes, he would throw himself into the deep water with a cry of delight. His father was a fisherman who owned his own little vineyard.

Boys grow apace and in a little while he was madly in love with a pretty girl. They became engaged, but they could not marry till Salvatore had done his military service, and when he left the island which he had never left in his life before, he wept like a child. It was hard for one who had never been less free than the birds to be at the beck and call of others; it was harder still to live in a battleship with strangers instead of in a little white cottage among the vines. He was dreadfully homesick. But it was hardest of all to be parted from the girl he loved with all his passionate young heart. He wrote letters in which he told her how much he longed to be back.

He fell ill of some mysterious ailment that kept him in hospital for months. When he learnt that it made him unfit for further service his heart exulted, for he could go home; and he scarcely listened, when the doctors told him that he would never again be quite well. What did he care when he was going back to the little island he loved so well and the girl who was waiting for him?

When he got into the rowing-boat that met the steamer and was rowed ashore he saw his father and mother standing on the jetty. His eyes searched among the crowd that waited there, for the girl. He could not see her. There was a great deal of kissing when he jumped up the steps. He asked where the girl was. His mother told him that she did not know; they had not seen her for two or three weeks; so in the evening when the moon was shining he walked down to her house. She was sitting on the doorstep with her mother. He was a little shy because he had not seen her for so long. He asked her if she had not received the letter he had written to her to say that he was coming home. Yes, they had received a letter, and they had been told by another of the island boys that he was ill. They had heard that he would never be quite well again. They were silent for a little, and then the mother nudged the girl. She did not try to soften the blow. She told him straight out, that she could not marry a man who would never be strong enough to work like a man. They had made up their minds.

When Salvatore went home he found that they all knew, but had lacked the courage to tell him themselves. He wept. He was terribly unhappy, but he did not blame the girl. A fisherman's life is hard, and he knew very well that a girl could not afford to marry a man who might not be able to support her. His smile was very sad, but he did not complain, and he never said a hard word of the girl he had loved so well. Then, a few months later, when he had settled down, working in his father's vineyard and fishing, his mother told him that there was a young woman willing to marry him. Her name was Assunta.

'She's as ugly as the devil,' he said.

She was older than he, and had been engaged to a man who had been killed while doing his military service. She had a little money of her own and if Salvatore married her she could buy him a boat of his own and they could take a vineyard that happened to be without a tenant. On the following Sunday he went to church and placed himself so that he could have a good look at the young woman. When he returned he told his mother that he was willing.

Well, they were married and settled down in a tiny white-washed house. Salvatore was now a great big husky fellow, tall, and broad, but still with that smile and those trusting, kindly eyes that he had had as a boy. Assunta had a good heart and she was no fool. She could not bear the girl who had thrown him over, and had nothing but harsh words for her. Presently children were born to them.

It was a hard enough life. He would set out in his boat or work in his vineyard.

Sometimes he used to bring his children down for a dip in the water. They were both boys and at this time the elder was three and the younger less than two. They sprawled about at the water's edge and Salvatore standing on a rock would dip them in the water. Salvatore had enormous hands, like legs of mutton, coarse and hard from constant toil, but when he bathed his children, holding them so tenderly, drying them with delicate care, upon my word they were like flowers. He would seat the baby on the palm of his hand and hold him up, laughing.

I started by saying that I wondered if I could do it and now I must tell you what it is that I have tried to do. I wanted to see whether I could hold your attention while I drew for you the portrait of a man who possessed nothing in the world except a quality which is the rarest, the most precious and the loveliest that anyone can have. And in case you have not guessed what the quality was, I will tell you. Goodness, just goodness.

Salvatore:
W. Somerset Maugham

Comment

The writer teases us at the beginning and end of his story. Before telling us about his hero, Salvatore, he presents himself with a challenge which we don't understand until his final paragraph; then the first sentence becomes clear. By this means he is able to give the story some shape.

Activities

– How did you feel when Salvatore was rejected by his first love? Do you think she was kind or cruel to tell him 'straight out' that she could not marry him? How else could she have told him? Note down your answers.
– Write 'A Day in the Life of Salvatore', as you imagine it to be. You could make the day before or after his marriage.
– A television producer aims to make some dramatizations of Somerset Maugham's short stories. You are his cameraman or woman and you have to list a sequence of shots for this story.
– The author writes, in his concluding paragraph, that it was his intention to draw in words the portrait of a man who showed goodness. Underline all the words, phrases, and sentences describing this goodness, or that show his likeable qualities.
– Write a short story that shows a person having one of these qualities: honesty, compassion, tolerance.

Nuts and Bolts

Nouns are used for naming. The commonest apply to things: roads, food, pens. The names of places and people are known as **proper nouns** because they are the property of someone or something, and they all begin with a **capital letter**: Sally, Scotland, Evans. Then there are **abstract nouns**, so called because they name qualities taken from a number of sources. The quality common to a number of fast cars is named by the abstract noun 'speed'; brave people share the quality 'bravery'; and so on. Many of these abstract nouns end in **-ness**. Now look at the very end of the piece and see how the story makes its point sharp and clear. Find the first proper noun in the unit.

This unit consists largely of short, clear, emphatic sentences. They make the story plain and enable it to be quickly taken in; the effect is gained by using plenty of full-stops. Choose a paragraph which illustrates this. Obviously you will not choose the last paragraph of all, because here Maugham writes longer sentences. He has stopped telling the tale and is thinking about it.

Think of three more words like 'pleasant' in which the **ea** sounds like 'e'. If you are stuck, think of the words for being in good physical condition, and for having a great deal of money.

Unit 4

A strong pong of grilled grill

Pete Williams, having done badly in some exams, is feeling rather sorry for himself. Sal is his sister:

After Sal had gone I switched off the door bell so that I shouldn't have to answer the door, then took the phone off the hook. I didn't feel like talking to anyone. I did think about ringing my friend Willie Trent, to see if he'd managed to do worse than I had, but he'd be bound to appear for he turned up at some time or other every day. Right at the moment I needed the security of my room, where things had been the same for a very long time, like the elderly blackamoor fish and two antique gerbils. One of them, Bert, could only just get up his little ladder, for he'd got arthritis in his back legs. Posters were peeling off the walls and the curtains had Noddy on them so they must have hung there for ages. I'd got records and cassettes and collections of comics piled everywhere. People told me they were appreciating in value but I just liked having them there along with old skateboards, old radios, old cameras and a whole load of Dinky toys. There I felt safe. I'd pulled round the bookcase so I could lie in bed with books at hand and my cassette player and not be seen from the doorway. Here was my space. A cavern of books and bits.

I put on an old punk recording just right for the way I felt that day, and sank down into the bed and into the music which took me and carried me away into wild space and the sound of the universe, where I could be free and untouched by people, be alone unto myself and unafraid.

I must have fallen asleep for I came to suddenly woken by the sound not of the universe but loud banging and roaring going on somewhere. I heaved myself off the bed in time to see Dad filling the doorway. Speaking.

'I come home early,' he was saying in a voice loud even for him, 'having spent my lunch-time beavering away on your behalf . . .'

'You needn't have bothered . . .' I began and then sniffed the air.

'Dad, what's that terrible smell?'

My father did a dance up and down in the doorway. For a big man he's light on his feet.

'Aha, so you noticed, did you? You're quick, I'll say that for you. In fact you amaze me. I never fail to be amazed at you through life, but today you have surpassed even yourself. "What's that smell?" you ask, standing there like a great goop. That smell, my boy, is the smell of the house burning.'

'The house burning?'

'You heard me. That's what I said. And you understood, did you? Clever boy.'

I managed to peer past him to a blue and smoke-filled landing. A strong pong of grilled grill was floating up the stairs.

'Hadn't we better do something?' I tried to push past him.

'Don't worry,' he said soothingly. 'It's all under control. But only because,' his voice started to get louder until it beat into my skull like hammer blows, 'I arrived home early full of peace and goodwill towards men, to find what? What indeed?' he bellowed, lowering his face close to mine. 'You might well ask. Half a dozen people crowding round the front door, its bell out of action, telephone engineers trampling all over the garden because the line's been reported out of order, and a fire engine screeching to a halt outside the house. Didn't you even hear that?'

I shook my head.

'The kitchen full of smoke and about to burst into flames!'

I tried to speak and couldn't.

'But don't worry about it. Don't give it a thought. It was just someone who shall be nameless, had left the grill on with toast under it, or what had been toast in earlier times . . .'

Oh, no, now I remembered.

'We were lucky the old bat next door noticed the smoke, tried to do something, found she couldn't get in and rang the fire brigade which is when I arrived, and I don't mean old bat, I mean dear old soul.'

'Is it all right? Is there much damage?'

'Not so much damage as I'd like to do to you, you incompetent nincompoop. The kitchen is greasy and smoky and filthy, the ceiling is black, the whole house reeks and the grill will never be the same again, but don't worry, it's all right, the house hasn't actually burnt down. We still have a roof over our heads. And I'm glad you got in a good morning's zizz, so essential to growing lads, because you're going to need all that energy for washing down walls and cleaning up.'

No Place Like:
Gene Kemp

Comment

Pete is unfortunate; his sister seems to be so much more successful than he is. His parents have differing views about him and his future, this extract showing quite clearly his father's attitude which, in the circumstances, we can well understand.

Activities

– Continue the extract for another four to five paragraphs.

– With the help of a friend, make a recording of the conversation between Pete and his father. Look closely at everything the father says so that you find just the right variety and tone. He doesn't, for example, rant and rave the whole time.

– Describe your bedroom. Does it resemble Pete's in any way? Do you look on your room as 'security'?

– Write a report for the fire brigade's incident book, as the senior fireman might have written it.

– This extract occurs near the beginning of the novel. Read the book to find out what happens to Pete.

Nuts and Bolts

There are some examples of **slang** in this piece, in the title and elsewhere. Find two of them. Slang gives vigour and liveliness to speech, but it is best kept for conversation. Slang words may be understood only in one area or by one group of people, and they tend to go out of date. However the best slang joins the language for regular use; 'hassle' for instance started as slang, but by now it is generally accepted.

Find the paragraph 'Aha, so you noticed . . .' and find in it a quotation of three words. Notice the rule for a **quotation within a quotation**; it has double quotation marks " . . .". But if the main quotation has double quotes, then the quote-within-a-quote will have single quotation marks ' . . .'.

Look at the final paragraph of the unit, and listen to it. Dad drives home the point by repeating the same type of sentence: 'The kitchen is . . . the ceiling is . . . the whole house . . . the grill will never . . .'.

The **ique** in 'unique' sounds like 'eek'. Find another word in the first paragraph with the same spelling for the same sound.

Unit 5

Vaulting ambition

It had to happen. Twelve years after a nation became besotted with a little Russian girl called Olga, and millions of girls across the country had set out to emulate her, a British gymnast has reached perfection, a feat that Olga Korbut herself never achieved: the glory of the perfect ten.

Britain's Little Miss Perfect is a chunky 15 year old called Jackie McCarthy, and she did it in a local competition, promptly turned red as a stop-light and then disappeared under a tidal wave of congratulating team mates. She did it with a vault – for the technically minded, it was a twisting tsukahara. And no one, said the mark, could have done it better.

The Loughton Gymnastics Club coach, Yvonne Arnold, competed alongside Olga in Munich. She says: 'The 12-year-old girls at this club can do more than I was able to do when I went to the Olympic Games. The progress we have made since then is unbelievable.' It is not just the British who have improved – it is the rest of the world as well. So many tens are being scored by the top gymnasts that the points scoring system is being changed.

Gymnastics has become a major sport in the West, not just in terms of participation, but in audience appeal – not just for the four-yearly thrash of the Olympics but also for ordinary events and displays in Britain.

Jackie is not, yet, a complete gymnast; not yet, despite the perfect ten, the perfect gymnast. She is a big-move specialist, not a graceful linker of moves. In the one event that is pure explosion, she excels.

She is a tumbler, 4ft 10in of tightly packed, bouncing energy. She is not one of your sinuous sylphs either: she is an up-and-at-'em competitor with the vaulting ambition of Macbeth and the steely nerves of a burglar.

In her repertoire of floor movements, she includes a double-back somersault with full twist, which is the hardest tumble performed by any girl in the world.

When it comes to tricks and fireworks, Jackie excels. The other side of the coin is that she finds compulsory exercises boring, and would rather work on a new and more exotic tumble. But in the Olympics and the World Championships, compulsories carry as many marks as the voluntary, firework-packed exercises. Perfect mark she may have, but she is no niggling perfectionist. She likes to learn new things, and keeps doing so, rather than perfecting her established moves. It's something that drives her coaches mad with mingled admiration and exasperation.

Her courage clearly worries her father Terry. 'I used to worry about her getting injured all the time – obviously I still do, but I don't feel I have to sit at home thinking, "When is that telephone going to ring?" I know the way they work on the moves, taking

them slowly, not taking chances.'

It can be disconcerting for parents to find an extraordinary and unsuspected talent emerging in their offspring. It can also be a relief for some gymnastic parents, who have found the undirected enthusiasms of their prodigy rather heavy on the furniture. 'Actually, Jackie wasn't like that,' says Terry. 'But she kept walking about on her hands all the time. Then one day her teacher said she wanted to see me. I thought she had managed to get herself into trouble. But no, the teacher said Jackie was showing lots of promise in gymnastics, and she ought to join a proper club. But I never expected her to do so well.'

Nor did Jackie herself. 'I wasn't that interested in gymnastics to start with – not until my second year.' And though everyone keeps enthusing about her speed in learning, she doesn't learn fast enough to please herself. 'Nothing is easy to learn,' she insists. 'It is only once you have learned something that it gets easy.'

Her enjoyment of the sport comes through despite the hard and unending labour of it all. 'The more you do, the more scared you get,' she says. 'But it is good to be scared. It means you don't take risks.' What, then, is the hardest part about gymnastics? She replies, candidly, 'I don't find anything hard.'

She is one of the many exceptional gymnasts now in Britain. The sport is improving by leaps and bounds, literally, with girls who have grace, talent and courage combined with the flawlessly focused desire to work and work on these natural abilities, to labour, and to answer the complex and dangerous demands of the sport. Has Jackie ever had a bad accident at gymnastics? 'Yes, once. I was competing in the vault, and my hand suddenly slipped on the horse. I landed flat on my back. I lost .5 of a mark.' That's serious.

From *Mail on Sunday*:
Simon Barnes

The Trampoline

'You can weigh what you like for a trampoline,
Dear Lady, for every additional ounce
The higher you go, if you see what I mean,
It's simply a question of bounce!
So here I go bouncing, dear lady, dear lady,
Bouncing, bouncing into the air.
You can land on your feet or alight on your bottom.
You soon get the knack of it. Never despair.
You can lilt like a lark in the morning, dear lady,
Or tumble and frolic and never feel sick.
All you must learn is the rhythm of bouncing,
Then you perform every kind of a trick,
You can swallow-dive, somersault, spring on your
palms,
You can dance funny dances aloft without qualms.
You can soar with the grace of a fairy queen,
Dear lady, you'll love the trampoline.'

John Pudney

Activities

– In spite of her achieving the perfect mark of ten, Jackie is not yet a complete or perfect gymnast. What faults does she have?
– Write Jackie's diary entry for the day she scored her ten.
– 'Nothing is easy to learn. It is only once you have learned something that it gets easy.' Has this been your experience – not necessarily in terms of sport? Write about something you found difficult at first, but now find easy.
– John Pudney's poem takes a somewhat light-hearted look at a trampoline lesson. Imagine the 'dear lady' climbing on to the trampoline for the first time. Write the account either from her point of view or as a spectator.
– 'The Competition.' Write about a competition in which you have taken part.
– Read 'The Artist', a poem by William Carlos Williams.

Nuts and Bolts

The second paragraph contains a **simile** and a **metaphor**, fairly close together. Similes usually start with 'like' or 'as'; and if you are not sure what a metaphor is, look at the expression 'firework-packed exercises'. There aren't any real fireworks in the exercises, only metaphorical ones, and the writer means that the exercises have the sparkle and brilliance of fireworks. We can always replace metaphors by simpler expressions, but they tend to be longwinded and less compact.

The **colon** (:) indicates that what follows is connected with what has just been said, so it is often used to introduce a list. We always put a colon when we introduce a unit; and you will find a good example in the first paragraph of the unit.

Later on in the piece you will see how the rule for quotations-within-quotations works; it was mentioned in Nuts and Bolts of Unit 4. Find the quotation in this unit.

What is noticeable about the spelling of: disappearance, unbelievable, relief and competitor? (NB It is different for each word.)

Unit 6

Escape from slavery

When the Romans withdrew their troops from Britain, a young cavalry officer, called Aquila, stayed behind with his farming family. But the ferocious Saxons invaded from Denmark, and he was captured and enslaved. One day he sees his sister Flavia in a Saxon town; she has been forced to marry a Saxon chief, and has had a child of his. They plan Aquila's escape after a feast when the Saxons are drunk; and now they meet:

'You have come, then,' she said, as he halted beside her.

It was such an obvious thing to say, but sometimes it was better to stick to the obvious things.

'I have come,' he said, and sent a swift glance towards the stockade gate, just visible in the mist. She saw the glance, and shook her head. 'There are none there to overhear us. Did I not say that I would take care of the guards on the shore-gate?'

There was a sudden chill in him. 'Flavia, you don't mean – what have you done to them?'

'Oh no, I am not a poisoner. They will but sleep a few hours.'

'But how –?' Aquila began, but she cut him short.

'It was a simple thing to do. They were glad enough of the mead cup that I brought down to them from Hengest's Hall. See now' – she brought a bundle from under her cloak – 'here is some food and a dagger, and a good sharp file that I stole. With the food, you can lie up for a day or so until you are free of that cruel thrall-ring, before you go among men again.'

Aquila took the bundle from her, mumbling something he did not know what. They stood looking at each other; and suddenly the ordinary things were no good, after all. . . .

'Come with me,' Aquila said – it felt like a sudden impulse, but he knew that it wasn't really.

'– and leave the babe?'

Silence again. Then Aquila said, 'Bring him too. We'll find somewhere – a place for ourselves. I'll work for both of you.'

'For the child of a Saxon father?'

Aquila looked down at the hand in which he held the bundle, and forced it to relax from the clenched and quivering fist that it had become. 'I will try to forget his Saxon father, and remember only that he is yours,' he said carefully.

She drew closer, lifting her face to his. It was very white in the moonlight and the wreathing mist; and her eyes had again that look of being mere black holes in the whiteness of it. 'Aquila, part of me would lie down and die tomorrow and not think it a heavy price to pay, if I might come with you tonight. But there's another part of me that can never come.'

'You mean, that you can't leave the man either.'

'Our Lord help me! He is *my* man.'

After a few moments she moved again, and held out something. 'You must go. But first – take this.'

'What is it?'

'Father's ring.'

Aquila made no move to take it. 'What will *he* do when he knows that you have given his bride gift away, and in what manner you gave it?'

'I shall tell him that I lost it.'

'And will he believe that?'

'Maybe not,' Flavia said. 'But he will not beat me.' How strange and luminous her eyes were, all at once, in the moonlight. 'I am quite safe, my dear. He is a brave man in his way, but he won't beat me.'

Aquila put his free hand on her shoulder, and looked down at her, trying to understand. 'Is it love, with you, or hate, Flavia?'

'I do not know. Something of both maybe, but it doesn't make any difference. I belong to him.' Her low voice was completely toneless. 'Take Father's ring, and – try to forgive me.'

He dropped his hand from her shoulder, and took the ring, and slid it on to his bare signet finger. The numbness that had helped him was wearing thin, and the black, appalling misery was aching through. Somewhere, hidden at the back of his mind, he had thought until now that she would come with him; he hadn't quite accepted that what had happened was for ever. He said in a voice as toneless as her own, 'If I escape by your help, and take Father's ring at your hands, then I must forgive you, Flavia.'

And without another word between them, they turned to the gateway. The guards lay tumbled beside it in uncouth attitudes, the mead cup between them; and Aquila was struck by a sudden fear – 'they'll tell, when they wake, who gave them the mead!'

'No,' Flavia said. 'The moon was not up then, and I took pains to change my voice. They will not know

who came.' She had gone to the bar that held the gate; but Aquila put her on one side, and raising the heavy timber himself, drew the gate open just enough to let him through. Then, in the narrow gap, he turned again to Flavia, for the last time; the last time of all. . . At the last moment he made a half-movement towards her; but she made none towards him, and he checked and let his arm fall to his side. 'God keep you, Flavia,' he said.

'And you,' Flavia whispered. 'God keep you always. Remember me sometimes – even though it hurts to remember.'

The Lantern Bearers: Rosemary Sutcliff

Comment

The 'thrall-ring' was a metal collar that the Saxons fixed round the neck of a slave. Flavia had been given her father's ring by the Saxon who destroyed her father's farm and took her for his wife.

The book paints a vivid picture of Britain under the Romans – its prosperity, for some, and then the violence and cruelty of the Saxon invasions – with a thrilling plot to match. The events described took place near the modern Richborough, on the north coast of Kent.

Activities

– 'How Aquila spent the next few hours.' Continue the story from where we finished, as you imagine it might have been.
– Do you think Flavia was right not to escape with her brother? Think of reasons both for her going and for her staying before you reach a decision.
– Flavia's husband discovers Aquila's escape. He questions her fiercely. Write a script of the dialogue as you imagine it.
– Find out (perhaps in a museum) where the nearest remains of the Roman occupation may be found. If you live within reach of London, visit the Museum of London at the Barbican.
– Try to find a map of Britain as it was under the Romans. Look at the main centres and the road system that connected them.
– Read *The Lantern Bearers*, or *The Eagle of the Ninth* by Rosemary Sutcliff.
– Search out a poem by Rudyard Kipling entitled 'The Roman Centurion's Song'. It is spoken by a Roman soldier who had been ordered back to Rome with his company and, just like Aquila, does not want to go. It ends with this request to his superior officer:

Legate, I come to you in tears – My cohort ordered home!
I've served in Britain forty years. What should I do in Rome?
Here is my heart, my soul, my mind – the only life I know.
I cannot leave it all behind. Command me not to go!

Nuts and Bolts

Prepositions are small words, usually placed in front of another word to show place, direction or manner: *in* the town, **to** the library, **with** a laugh. In the paragraph 'I have come . . .' the first two prepositions are 'towards' and 'in'. Find two more near the end of the same paragraph.

In the paragraph 'Aquila took . . .' 'mumbled' is exactly the right word to describe the way he spoke. Look for two more precisely right words in the next twenty-five lines.

When Flavia says 'He is *my* man' *my* is printed in *italics* for emphasis.

Look at each of these words steadily for a moment, and then say them: vis*ible*, beli*eve*, lumin*ous*, *app*alling, a*ch*ing. Why have we put parts of the words in italics?

Unit 7

Like words, hate words, calm words

Words can be very powerful. They have stirred men and women to do heroic deeds and lose their lives; they have moved mobs to commit acts of madness and cruelty. But words work that way in everyday life as well as on big occasions. Our feelings are there all the time, just below the surface and always ready to erupt. Sometimes it is friendliness and affection, and sometimes it is hatred and contempt that are ready to surface. These feelings produce what we call 'like' words and 'hate' words – or 'snarl' words. In between there are 'calm' words.

For instance, a policeman can be referred to in three ways. In a newspaper report he is a 'police constable'; those are calm words, quite neutral words. He – or she – can also be a 'copper' or 'bobby'; those are 'like' words, because they show that the user has friendly feelings towards the police and is on their side. Thirdly, he is sometimes called 'the fuzz', and other terms which show that the speaker dislikes the police and is not on their side; here, he is using 'hate' words.

Again, 'black' and 'negro' are calm words; they just refer to people of a particular race. But if we say 'nigger' we add dislike and scorn to the meaning. 'Nigger' is a hate word and shows that the person using it has lost his power of thinking fairly. He is prejudiced, as we nearly all are in one way or another. To make sure you've got the idea, try replacing these hate words by calm words: egg-head, yid, Red, tripper, dago. On the other hand think of the animal words that show the speaker's affection and approval: ducks or ducky, chick, lamb, bird, bunny, kittenish. There are also animal words for dislike and disapproval: donkey, pig, cow, swine, goose, rabbit, cur, catty.

If you are in doubt about anything so far in this unit, reread carefully. The point we are anxious to make clear is that words can be used in two ways.

'. . . they have moved mobs to commit acts of madness and cruelty.'

First, to tell us facts in a calm objective way. Secondly, to show our feelings about someone or something, and get other people to share those feelings. This should not be difficult to understand, because you are a human being like the rest of us and will use words in these two ways every day of your life. Text books, especially in a science subject, will always make use of words in a calm objective way, whereas a story or a poem or newspaper article will be full of terms that tell us what the author feels about things.

Read this description of a golden eagle:

This great bird, with its magnificent flight, is seldom seen except in North Scotland, where it still breeds. The plumage is dark brown, with golden-brown on the head and nape. The feathers on the legs distinguish it from the Sea-Eagle. Immature birds have a wide white band across the base of the tail. The female is three inches longer than the male.

That is a concise description from a biologist's point of view of the bird's appearance, size and habitat.

Next read this poem by Tennyson:

The Eagle

He clasps the crag with hookéd hands;
Close to the sun in lonely lands,
Ringed with the azure world, he stands.

The wrinkled sea beneath him crawls;
He watches from his mountain walls,
And like a thunderbolt he falls.

Read the poem again, if possible aloud. This will help to bring out the meaning – the way in which those hard 'K' sounds at the beginning convey the hardness of the rocks clutched by the eagle's claws, and the speed of the last short line. Make sure you understand 'hooked' and why from the bird's viewpoint the sea is 'wrinkled' and 'crawls'. The whole poem gives us an impression of the majesty and power of the eagle and the lonely heights where it makes its home.

The two pieces are different because the writers have different purposes. It is interesting that the writer of the first piece cannot resist using one word that tells us little about the eagle, but does reveal what the biologist feels about it. The word is near the beginning.

Almost any newspaper or magazine will supply examples of the way in which the aims of writers influence their choice of words. Some of the newspages and the accounts of sporting events will aim at describing what happened for those of us who were not present. On the other hand the articles about politics and the displayed advertisements will try to influence our feelings by their choice of words. A full-page advertisement for a car will go on about its sporting performance, its looks, its luxury, and its superiority to other vehicles, but important information, such as the actual price will be in minute print, if it is there at all. And once our feelings are affected, we are likely to spend our money or cast our votes as someone else wants us to.

Activities

– Look at an article in a daily newspaper expressing opinion. Read through the article carefully, underlining any *like* and *hate* words.
– Consult a dictionary for the words in italics:

I am *firm*
you are *obstinate*
he is *pig-headed*

Do the words mean the same thing? You should have two answers.
– One of the hardest aspects of learning a foreign language is to judge accurately the *emotional* meaning of words. (The use of gesture and facial expression has to be learnt, too.) Write a short story in which someone learning English as a foreign language uses the word 'immediately' with a stern face, instead of 'now' with a questioning smile.
– Take a newspaper article in which the newspaper's viewpoint is clearly on one side (about a terrorist bomb attack, perhaps – and that isn't a *neutral* statement, as we have used the word 'terrorist') and re-write it from the opposing view.
– Make a list of words that describe character (for example, affable, arrogant, impatient) and place them on a chart set out like this:

Like words	*Calm words*	*Hate words*

Nuts and Bolts

Take any two paragraphs in the unit and see if the opening sentence of each gives a good idea of the rest of the paragraph.

The words in each of these pairs mean the same, but one is calm, and the other a word showing the speaker's feelings. Say which is the calm word:

non-striker, scab
conchie, pacifist
communist, bolshie
tactless, outspoken
error, blunder
taciturn, reserved

The word 'advertisement' near the end comes from the verb 'advertise'. Some of these *-ise* words can also be spelled with *-ize*. We recommend that you stick to -*ise*; to spell some of the words with a 'z' can cause unnecessary confusion.

Unit 8

The adventure was over

Forrest is persuaded by his friend Alan to join him in breaking into a house. As soon as they are in, Forrest is ashamed; the adventure is not in his line, and he just wants to get out. Horror seizes him when he sees a human foot sticking out from under a bed, but it is only a boot:

I waited here until Alan should have finished, and a sense of unhappiness and disillusionment swept over me, shutting out everything else. Even had I seen a ghost ascending the stairs, or heard the sound of someone at the hall-door, I do not think I should have cared. What I knew as I hung there over the banisters in the soft grey darkness, was that I was far enough now from my dream place, and that the figure I had left in the room behind me, moving swiftly and stealthily hither and thither, searching and prying, ransacking drawers and cupboards, was far enough removed from my dream playmate.

Presently I came back to the open door, and as I did so I saw him slip something into his pocket. I watched him without surprise. It was as if I had come back expecting to see just this, for even out there on the landing I had known that everything was at an end . . .

'You can't do that,' I said quietly.

'Do what?' he answered.

'You can't take anything.'

He turned round and looked at me. 'Why?' he asked.

'Because – these things don't belong to you.'

He paused. 'All right,' he said at last. 'Don't worry. I'll put it back.'

'On your honour, you won't take anything?'

'On my honour . . . But it's rather a waste, isn't it?'

'You don't mean to say you intended to take anything?' I asked, with a sudden suspicion of the truth. 'I mean, it wasn't for that you wanted to get in?'

'I know it's quite different from robbing a fruit garden,' he said, with a faint sneer.

'It is different,' I answered. 'And it's rotten – rotten even to poke about among other people's things the way you've been doing.'

He remained silent for a moment or two, while an unpleasant expression came into his face. 'I'd forgotten you were such a saint – when it comes to doing things you don't want to do.'

'Shall we go?' I suggested.

He hesitated again . . . 'There's a soft streak in you somewhere. I can't quite make out what it is, but I've noticed it before.'

'You didn't tell me.'

'No, but I've noticed it . . . Just now when you came into the room, too, you looked as if you were going to cry.'

I had begun to feel profoundly miserable. 'It wasn't, anyway, about what you think,' I muttered. 'It was something else.'

'What?'

'I don't know.'

And really, I didn't know. At all events I could not tell him. We descended the staircase and let ourselves out at the back. The adventure was over.

But as I walked beside him everything was altered. It was as if I had emerged from some spellbound wood into a disenchanted land in which I saw things exactly as they were. And it was in this cold and rather dreary light that I saw the boy beside me, nor could I even understand what I had before found so attractive about him. Yet only two evenings ago I had been on the point of pouring all my confidences into his ear! For this escape at least I was thankful. And I wondered, as we walked home together, if he had

really put back everything as he had promised to do. I do not think he had, but perhaps I was wrong. Our remarks became more perfunctory, and when we reached the gate we paused and faced each other across the wooden bars, for he had not asked me to come in.

'What's the matter with you?' he said abruptly.

I pretended to be surprised. 'With me? Nothing.'

There was silence, and I fancy he knew, as I certainly knew, that we should not see each other again. We said goodnight, and I turned on down the road towards my own home.

The twilight was gone. A thin silver moon had risen above the motionless trees, and though I was already late I sat down on a bank under a garden hedge, through which there came a penetrating sweetness – the scent of mignonette.

Apostate:
Forrest Reid

Comment

In several of our units the authors have pictured themselves as rather unpleasant children. As we read the extracts, we feel that the authors, being good at writing, have taken the opportunity to exaggerate a bit, in order to produce something interesting and entertaining. Forrest Reid is telling us about his childhood, but he does not make himself out to be worse than he was; there's no sign that he was a burglar in the making. He was looking for adventure, rather than plunder. However breaking into a house was carrying the search for adventure rather too far, as he himself realized.

The moon, the still trees and the sweet scent form a peaceful natural scene, which is to Forrest a reminder – a reminder that there are more important and more permanent things than a passing whim like the quest for adventure.

Activities

– Most of us have done something or started something about which we felt thoroughly ashamed when we thought more about it. Think of an occasion when this happened to you. You could turn your experience into a short story, changing your name, if you wish, to make it impersonal.

– Alan and Forrest broke in for quite different reasons. What were they?

– Forrest sits down in his bedroom sometime later to write his thoughts about the escapade in his diary. What does he write?

– Describe a day in the life of Alan a year or two after this incident.

– It has been suggested that there is little scope in modern life for adventure. Do you agree? What possibilities are there for you?

– Try *John Macnab* by John Buchan. It is a story about a hunting and fishing adventure, with high reputations at stake.

– Do you know any people whose home has been broken into? Ask them about their feelings when they discovered it.

Nuts and Bolts

Note at the end of the first paragraph how successfully the writer gives the impression of a thief at work by choosing words with pulling power. Pick out the words you find effective; there is no need to write them.

How does the final paragraph supply a contrast to the rest of the piece?

Words ending in **-et** or **-ette**, like 'mignonette', originally indicated small size; 'cigarette' once meant a small cigar. Think of three more words with the **-et** or **-ette** ending; if in doubt think of tapes and cinemas and eggs.

Unit 9

Indian girl and English boy

Ralph's going to be an actor. He always gets the highest marks in English and takes over the drama class when he's feeling like it. He's clever. He can play the guitar and I think he tries to look like a pop star, with shaded glasses and a sort of smart haircut, long at the back and short on top. He brings the best records to school, not all that reggae rubbish and Donny Osmond and Slade. He listens to David Bowie and the Rolling Stones and all sorts of new groups that no one's ever heard of. He says he's learning to play the sitar from the lead guitarist of a group he's going to join.

One day, about a week ago, he said he wanted to listen to some Hindi pop and I said my dad's only got film songs and he gets them straight from India so he won't let them out of his sight. 'In that case I'll have to listen to them in your house, won't I?' he said.

To tell you the truth, I was very glad he said that and I told him I'd tell him when he could come because my dad had to be got in the right mood. If Ralph came too often he'd start getting ideas and making a fuss.

I talk to my nan about my friends, so I told her about Ralph and she asked if he was from a good family and whether I liked him. I said that I did like him a little, and there weren't any good or bad families in Britain, they were all the same. She said that that could never be, there was always a difference between gold and lead and the older you get the better you could tell.

My dad has the same sort of ideas. You can't blame him because he must have got them from her. He lectures us on and on about such things. When we went to pick up Nan from the airport, he was saying he hadn't lost respect for his own dad, even though he was dead. My brother's quite cheeky and he said, 'Neither did Hamlet,' but my dad doesn't understand about Shakespeare so the joke was no good on him.

Dad always says that English people put their parents in old people's homes because they have no shame, but we Indians know how to look after our own. Sometimes when he talks that way I like it, it makes me feel different and also better than the rest, because it's true I suppose, they don't have any old folk's homes in India. But there are beggars and hungry people all about the streets and when I point that out my dad says it's true, but what can one do, there are rich and poor everywhere and poor people may be starving but they have good hearts.

'Can't pay the rent with good hearts,' my brother says.

When Dad speaks like this it frightens me too, because I don't really know anything about India. Since I was four I've lived in London and now that I'm fifteen I often think of going to India. My mother always says we're going next year, but dad says there's not enough money saved and next year never comes. If I start earning my own money I'll save up and go, just for a visit.

The day Ralph came Dad was on the evening shift. Ralph turned up, as always with books and LPs in his hand. We sat in the front room where the record player was and where Mum could have kept an eye on us while she cooked next door in the kitchen. Ralph had been there a few times and he always sat politely, not like at school where he sprawls out on the desks and sits with his trousers pulled to his shins, cross-legged on the cement flower-pots in the school playground.

Nan was in the house when he arrived, and Mum had just nipped out to the launderette with two loads. Nan came and sat in the front room with us while we played the discs and talked in English. I kept watching the door for Dad, knowing it wouldn't really matter, if Nan was in the same room. She wanted to know why Ralph wore a necklace – he had a chain and pendant, the sort you buy for a few bob in Shepherds Bush Market. . . .

After we played through some of Dad's LPs, Ralph wanted to put on his own and asked if it was all right. 'There are Indian bells on this one, remind you of the cows tinkling home in the sunset, listen,' he said.

Now I don't listen much to pop, but I was relieved that Dad wouldn't come home to find us playing with his records. So Ralph put on the Stones and we listened. We sat through it and talked. Then he said, 'What about all the old Indian hospitality then, you haven't even offered me a bleeding cup of tea?'

I wish he hadn't said that, because I didn't want to ask Nan to make it and if Mum had been there it would have been all right, but according to Hindu custom you only serve up tea to a young man when your dad has brought him home to look you over as a marriage proposition. I said to Nan that there were cokes in the fridge and she got the hint and perhaps she understood that it was awkward for me so she went and got them herself and she did a very sweet thing, she brought them on a tray with a can-opener. Ralph said it was a good idea and began to open the can with the can-opener and I split myself laughing because Nan didn't understand what she had done wrong. She began talking to Ralph in Gujerati as though he understood every word and he just smiled at her.

East End at Your Feet:
Farrukh Dhondy

Comment

This unit shows up very sharply the different ways in which friendships are formed in India and England – at least in one part of it. The English boy models behaviour on films and the pop stars in fashion at the moment; but in India traditional customs decide the behaviour expected of a boy.

A sitar is an Indian musical instrument, rather like a lute or guitar, but with seven strings and a longer neck.

Activities

– What signs are there that the girl who tells the story is becoming westernized?
– Ask an Indian, or other non-native person, about the main differences between life in his or her homeland and Britain.
– One difference between the Indian and British ways of life is that in India much more seems to be decided for the individual than it is in Britain. Are there advantages in having less choice?
– Ralph's behaviour at school is different from when he visits the girl. Do you behave differently at school? Do your friends? Why do you think this is often the case?
– Imagine the girl's father coming home when Ralph is there. Write the dialogue as Ralph is introduced.
– Read E.R. Braithwaite's *To Sir, With Love.*
– What had Hamlet to do for his father in the play of that name?

Nuts and Bolts

Look at the words with **apostrophes** in the first two paragraphs and think in each case what the full form would be. Then read the little paragraph 'After we played through . . .' near the end to find another use of the apostrophe; and think what it is for. Remember that dog**'s** bones refers to one dog, while dogs**'** bones means there is more than one animal.

These small marks can matter. There is an apostrophe missing somewhere in 'Those things over there are my husbands'. Where should it go?

Unit 10

His first flight

The young seagull was alone on his ledge. His two brothers and his sister had flown away the day before. He had been afraid to fly with them. Somehow when he had taken a little run forward to the brink of the ledge and attempted to flap his wings he became afraid. The great expanse of sea stretched down beneath, and it was such a long way down – miles down.

He felt certain that his wings would never support him, so he bent his head and ran away back to the little hole under the ledge where he slept at night. Even when each of his brothers and his little sister, whose wings were far shorter than his own, ran to the brink, flapped their wings and flew away he failed to muster up courage to take that plunge which appeared to him so desperate. His father and mother had come around calling to him shrilly, upbraiding him, threatening to let him starve on his ledge unless he flew away. But for the life of him he could not move . . .

The sun was now ascending the sky, blazing warmly on his ledge that faced the south. He felt the heat because he had not eaten since the previous night-fall. Then he had found a dried piece of mackerel's tail at the far end of his ledge. Now there was not a single scrap of food left. He had searched every inch, rooting among the rough, dirt-caked straw nest where he and his brothers and sister had been hatched. He even gnawed at the dried pieces of spotted eggshell. It was like eating part of himself. He had then trotted back and forth from one end of the ledge to the other, his grey body the colour of the cliff, his long grey legs stepping daintily, trying to find some means of reaching his parents without having to fly. But on each side of him the ledge ended in a sheer fall of precipice, with the sea beneath. And between him and his parents there was a deep, wide chasm. Surely he could reach them without flying if he could move northwards along the cliff face? But then on what could he walk? There was no ledge, and he was not a fly. And above him he could see nothing. The precipice was sheer, and the top of it was perhaps farther away than the sea beneath him.

He stepped slowly out to the brink of the ledge, and, standing on one leg with the other leg hidden under his wing, he closed one eye, then the other, and pretended to be falling asleep. Still they took no notice of him. He saw his two brothers and his sister lying on the plateau dozing, with their heads sunk into their necks. His father was preening his feathers on his

white back. Only his mother was looking at him. She was standing on a little high hump on the plateau, her white breast thrust forward. Now and again she tore at a piece of fish that lay at her feet, and then scraped each side of her beak on the rock. The sight of the food maddened him. How he loved to tear food that way, scraping his beak now and then to whet it! He uttered a low cackle. His mother cackled too, and looked over at him.

'Ga, ga, ga,' he cried, begging her to bring him over some food. 'Gaw-ool-ah,' she screamed back derisively. But he kept calling plaintively, and after a minute or so he uttered a joyful scream. His mother had picked up a piece of fish and was flying across to him with it. He leaned out eagerly, tapping the rock with his feet, trying to get nearer to her as she flew across. But when she was just opposite to him, abreast of the ledge, she halted, her legs hanging limp, her wings motionless, the piece of fish in her beak almost within reach of his beak. He waited a moment in surprise, wondering why she did not come nearer, and then, maddened by hunger, he dived at the fish. With a loud scream he fell outwards and downwards into space. His mother had swooped upwards. As he passed beneath her he heard the swish of her wings. Then a monstrous terror seized him and his heart stood still. He could hear nothing. But it only lasted a moment. The next moment he felt his wings spread outwards. The wind rushed against his breast feathers, then under his stomach and against his wings. He could feel the tips of his wings cutting through the air. He was not falling headlong now. He was soaring gradually downwards and outwards. He uttered a joyous scream and flapped them again. He soared higher. He raised his breast and banked against the wind. 'Ga, ga, ga. Ga, ga, ga. Gaw-ool-ah.' His mother swooped past him, her wings making a loud noise. He answered her with another scream. Then his father flew over him screaming. Then he saw his two brothers and his sister flying around him curveting and banking and soaring and diving. . .

He was near the sea now, flying straight over it, facing straight out over the ocean. He saw a vast green sea beneath him, with little ridges moving over it, and he turned his beak sideways and crowed amusedly. His parents and his brothers and sister had landed on the green floor in front of him. They were beckoning to him, calling shrilly. He dropped his legs to stand on the green sea. His legs sank into it. He screamed with fright and attempted to rise again, flapping his wings. But he was tired and weak with hunger and he could not rise, exhausted with the strange exercise. His feet sank into the green sea, and then his belly touched and he sank no farther. He was floating on it. And around him his family were screaming, praising him, and their beaks were offering him scraps of dogfish.

He had made his first flight.

Short Stories:
Liam O'Flaherty

Comment

Liam O'Flaherty was born in the Aran Islands, off the west coast of Ireland, and wrote novels and many short stories.

You may remember *Jonathan Livingston Seagull* in Volume 1 of this series. Though both are about seagulls, the tales are quite different. The earlier one was a fable, that is a story about animals which think and behave like human beings, the author's aim being to tell us something about people. The one you've just read is about a gull and nothing else; the author aims at describing how the bird might have felt in facing and surmounting a difficulty.

Activities

– Can you remember being held up by nerves or fear when faced by a difficulty, and then overcoming it? Say what happened.
– Write a story about an equally important event in the life of some other living creature.
– Find out about sea-birds and waders. How is it that a gull's plumage does not become water-logged? And how can a wading bird survive in freezing water that would kill a man?
– If you live near the sea, you may have heard that gulls are a problem to some coastal towns. Describe the problem and say what some places are doing about it.
– Write a poem about the gull from the moment it dived out from the cliff at the fish. Refresh your memory about writing in free verse by re-reading Unit 17, 'Snake', in Volume 2.
– Use your dictionary to make sure of the meanings of: upbraid, whet, derisively, plaintively.

Nuts and Bolts

At the end of the second paragraph we read 'For the life of him he could not move' – meaning 'Even to save his life, he . . .'. This is an example of an **idiom**, a way of expressing that specially belongs to the English language. Later on there is another: 'his heart stood still'; what does this mean?

'Dirt-caked' shows the use of a **hyphen** to join two words to convey one idea. When two words are regularly used together, the hyphen is dropped, as in 'eggshell'. Find another hyphenated pair, near the end. Some pairs, like 'bus-stop', are unlikely to be made into one word, because we have to make a pause between the two in saying them.

In looking at **ie** words we refer to the **I before E** rhyme:

I before E
(except after C)
if the sound is EE.

'Seized' is the one important exception to the rule and must be learned. Link it with 'Sheila'.

Unit 11

More heat than light

Kate and her father quarrelled about once a month on average. It was usually over something trivial. They loved each other dearly and often found each other irritating.

Edward Milbank sometimes described his daughter as bright and bossy. Kate admitted she was bright but denied that she was bossy. Actually Edward was right: Kate *was* bossy. It was mostly because she had considered herself to be in charge of the household since she was twelve, which was nearly five years previously.

Let's begin with Edward. He was tall and thin, with wavy silver-grey hair. He looked distinguished. When people met him for the first time, they often thought they'd seen him before, or at any rate heard of him; and so they had. This wasn't because of his job as Foreign Editor of a London newspaper. It was because he appeared briefly on television from time to time, to be consulted about the significance of events in some country that had come into bad news. Not that Essenheim ever came into the news. Nothing happened in Essenheim to interest the rest of the world until Kate went there.

Kate's quarrel with Edward had been going on all week. Until the day of Susan's party it was conducted by correspondence. This was because, five days a week, Edward and Kate didn't see each other. Kate got up at half-past seven and left for school soon after eight. Edward got up at noon, made himself some lunch, listened to the radio news, read a pile of daily newspapers, and went to work at three. Kate came home from school at four, did her homework, read, watched television, and went to bed about eleven. Edward came home at half-past one, wound down with a novel and a couple of small whiskies, and went to bed at three. Kate got up at half-past seven and the cycle continued.

This may sound an odd way of life, but it's not unusual in households with a newspaperman in them. In fact it was really why Edward's marriage had broken down. Anne Milbank had complained bitterly about staying at home five nights a week with only a child for company. In the end she'd met someone who worked less unsocial hours and gone off with him, leaving Kate and her father together.

After that happened, Edward had got himself on to day work for a year or two, but he was back on nights now. And during the week, when he and Kate had things to say to each other, they left notes. Edward's

job on the *Morning Intelligence* involved a lot of decision-making on questions such as whether to spend large amounts of the paper's money sending reporters on overseas assignments, or whether to print reports that might lead to diplomatic crises. When he got home the last thing he wanted to do was make decisions. So Kate had gradually taken over the management of the house. She did the shopping and organized the repairs and replacements. If a room needed decorating, Kate decorated it, and Edward didn't even notice it had been done.

Anyway, on Monday night that week Kate left a note for Edward. It asked, coldly, '*Must* you leave dirty saucepans around and crumbs on the carpet?' On Tuesday morning she found a reply scrawled at the foot of her note saying, 'In yesterday's circumstances, yes.' On Tuesday night Kate inquired, '*What* circumstances?' On Wednesday morning the note was still there, with no further comment from Edward. Actually he hadn't seen it.

On Wednesday afternoon Kate had a tiresome interview at school about the subjects she was to do next year; then she had to go and buy some cleaning materials for the house. She was hot and cross and just in the mood to be irritated all over again. So underneath the words '*What* circumstances?' which she'd written the previous night, she added a row of five question marks, each bigger than the last, followed by an enormous exclamation mark; and she put the note where Edward couldn't fail to find it, under the coffee-pot.

On Thursday morning she found that Edward had added the one word 'Crisis'. On Thursday night she wrote crossly beneath this, '*What* crisis?' On Friday morning the note still lay on the kitchen table, with the further message, 'Can't remember now. Too much water under the bridge.' On Friday night Kate filled the remaining space on the scrap of paper, which by now was a bit grubby and smeared with marmalade, with the words 'Oh, you are *hopeless*!' And on Saturday afternoon, when at last they were at home together, they had a row.

Like all such rows, this one generated more heat than light. Old grievances were brought out and old accusations thrown around. It was all made worse by the fact that Kate and Edward were so involved with each other emotionally. Otherwise they wouldn't have been so nasty over something so unimportant. Kate claimed that she worked her fingers to the bone for an unhelpful and unappreciative father. Edward claimed that he risked heart failure or nervous breakdown in a gruelling job to support a nagging and bad-tempered child. And so on. In the end, Kate declared that she was longing for the day when she could leave home, and Edward proclaimed that it couldn't come too soon for him. Both statements were untrue, but that didn't prevent them from hurting.

At about tea-time the battle ended, both sides having run out of ammunition. But neither of them was ready yet to make peace. Kate having said she would never speak to her father again, and Edward having indicated that this would be no hardship, a long and heavy silence fell between them. And in mid-evening Kate announced that she would go to Susan Baker's party after all.

A Foreign Affair:
John Rowe Townsend

Comment

Kate meets a handsome young foreigner, who is heir to the throne of a tiny little independent state in Eastern Europe, and through him visits his country and gets tangled in the sometimes violent politics of the little place. This extract comes from the novel's opening chapter.

Activities

– How do you think Kate enjoyed herself at Susan Baker's party? From what you know of her character in this extract, would the row have lingered on in her mind, preventing enjoyment?

– Write Kate's diary entry for the Saturday.

– There can be very few teenagers who have not had disagreements with their parents, usually over trivial matters that loom up out of all proportion. Thinking back over such a disagreement, and writing it down either as a factual account or by fictionalizing it, can often help us to see matters in perspective. By using words, we come to control our thoughts and feelings. Writing 'Temper', the poem in Unit 44 of Volume 1, probably helped its young author to understand himself better.

Think back over the last month or two to see if there is an incident you would like to reflect upon and turn into a poem, a straightforward account, or a short story.

– As a title for this unit, we chose a phrase from the beginning of the penultimate paragraph, 'more heat than light'. Work out an alternative title which summarizes the extract.

– Imagine you are one of Kate's friends to whom she has written a letter giving an account of the episode. Write a reply offering her consolation and advice.

Nuts and Bolts

Find the fifth paragraph 'This may sound . . .'. Write down the four sentences on separate lines, but in a different order.

Look back to the jumbled paragraph you wrote out in Unit 2 and reassemble the sentences in the right order.

In the last paragraph but two, what is the meaning of the **idiom** 'too much water under the bridge'?

To which of these words in the unit does the **I before E** rule not apply: briefly, foreign, grievance? Don't just guess; think of the reason.

'Organize' can also be spelled with an *s*.

Unit 12

Thank you

Dear Uncle Arthur,

Thank you for your extremely generous Christmas present. I don't know how you guessed, but socks were exactly what I wanted.

What socks, too! I have looked it up and see that it is the Macpherson tartan. And how clever of you to remember that I take size seven.

* * *

Dear Aunt Millie,

How very kind of you to remember me at Christmas! And with socks too! In fact socks were quite the nicest present I received – size ten was just right, and the very delicate mauve will go excellently with a yellow suit. I must try to get one.

* * *

Dear Mrs Thimble,

I can't tell you how touched I am that you still go on remembering us 'children' (as I suppose you still think of us!) every year. And socks were just what I needed. I particularly like the pretty blue ribbons they do up with – they match perfectly the bluebells on the matinee jacket you gave me last Christmas. I shall certainly think of you every time I wear them.

* * *

Dear Great-Uncle Alexander,

I scarcely know what to say! I must admit I had been secretly hoping that someone would give me socks – and you did! Socks are always handy to have – and yours were so cleverly and appropriately Christmassy. I don't think I have ever seen socks with a pattern of holly and mistletoe before, though my favourites are the 'Yuletide Lafter' pair. Some of the jokes printed on them are almost too good to keep hidden under one's trouser-leg!

* * *

Dear Great-Aunt Tilly,

I must write at once to thank you for your magnificent present. I can't tell you what my feelings were when I opened that huge parcel and found it contained – a pair of socks!

It was very clever of you to choose a pair with one red and one grey. They make a great change from the ordinary run of socks, and I shall keep them for very special occasions. And how thoughtful of you to remember that my right foot it two inches longer than my left!

I hope you haven't been having any more trouble with your eyesight recently.

* * *

Dear Aunt Clara,

Socks! I scarcely know what to say! What ever should I do without my annual supply of socks from you? I suppose I ought really to thank Aunt Millie, who first put the idea into your head fifteen years ago by showing you that snapshot of me on a Scout hike. Yes, as you say, a Boy Scout can always do with another pair of socks.

I was very struck by the pattern. As you know, I have distant American connections on my Mother's side, so the stars and stripes motif is particularly suitable.

* * *

Dear Aunt Lou,

I scarcely know what to say! Socks! Well, what a surprise!

I'm particularly touched because I can see at a glance that they're home-knitted. You can't buy socks like that in the shops! They never manage to get the heel quite as comfortably far forward on shop-bought socks as you have, and they always make them so ridiculously tightly knit. You can suffocate a foot without plenty of air-spaces in the sock.

How did you guess I took size fifteen?

* * * * *

Dear Cousin Harry

Many happy returns! I hope you'll forgive the present – it's not easy shopping for a birthday present just after Christmas. But remembering your penchant for Burns I thought you might be rather amused by a pair of tartan socks.

I believe it's Uncle Ned's birthday next week, too. Do you think he'd like a pair of socks? I've seen a pale mauve pair that might take his fancy – or a big hand-knitted pair with sort of peep holes in them that would also do as Balaclava helmets. As I always say, socks invariably come in handy one way or another.

Dear Cousin Harry,

Many happy returns! I hope you'll forgive the present – it's not easy shopping for a birthday present just after Christmas. But remembering your penchant for Burns I thought you might be rather amused by a pair of tartan socks.

I believe it's Uncle Ned's birthday next week, too. Do you think he'd like a pair of socks? I've seen a pale mauve pair that might take his fancy – or a big hand-knitted pair with sort of peep-holes in them that would also do as Balaclava helmets. As I always say, socks invariably come in handy, one way or another.

The Book of Fub:
Michael Frayn

Comment

You probably didn't find the first letter very funny. The letters become funny only when you realize that the writer had socks for Christmas – and nothing else. What else in the letters makes us laugh? There are several possible reasons: the socks are different sizes (from seven to fifteen), their colours and designs are rather unusual – or they have various faults ('hand-knitted pair with sort of peep-holes'). The climax occurs when you come to the last letter, which is most unexpected; the writer had found an ingenious way of disposing of the socks.

Activities

– Imagine you are the writer of these letters, opening your presents on Christmas morning. Describe your thoughts as you tear open each parcel and see that you have been given – socks.
– Write Cousin Harry's thank-you letter.
– Imagine that two people have given you the same record or cassette. You decide whose record to keep, and that thank-you letter is easy to write. But what do you say to the other giver? Try writing the letter.
– Read the letters out to someone who has a good sense of humour. Did you laugh in the same places, or do different people find different things funny?
– Choose one of the characters who sent the socks and imagine the character's thoughts as he or she sits down to decide what presents to give.

Nuts and Bolts

The humour of this unit depends partly on the **double meaning** of so much of it. Find one example of something which can be taken in two ways.

Hyphens are used here to make two words convey one idea: great-uncle, trouser-leg. Find two more examples of this use. A hyphen can be useful in avoiding confusion. There was trouble when a newspaper missed out a hyphen and reported that 'Twenty odd people attended the meeting . . .'.

There are several **adverbs** in the unit, some formed just by adding **-ly** to an adjective, as in 'extremely'. What happens with 'comfortable' and 'invariable'?

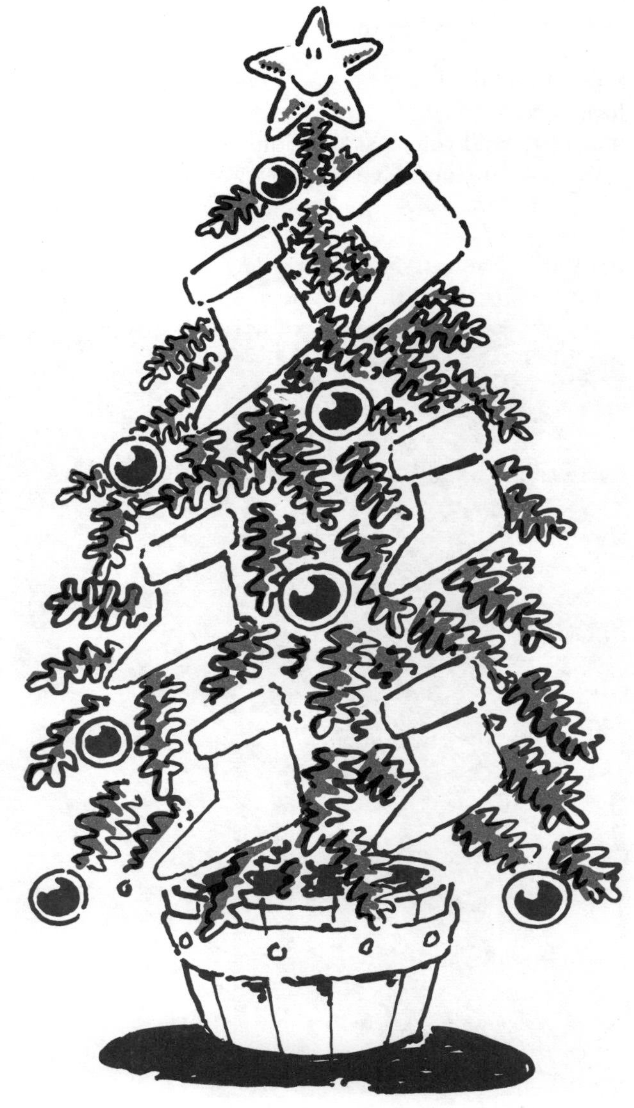

Unit 13

Last to go

A coffee stall, a BARMAN and an old NEWSPAPER SELLER. The BARMAN leans on his counter, the OLD MAN stands with tea.

Silence.

MAN: You was a bit busier earlier.
BARMAN: Ah!
MAN: Round about ten.
BARMAN: Ten, was it?
MAN: About then.
Pause.
I passed by here about then.
BARMAN: Oh yes?
MAN: I noticed you were doing a bit of trade.
Pause.
BARMAN: Yes, trade was very brisk here about ten.
MAN: Yes, I noticed.
Pause.
MAN: I sold my last one about then. Yes. About nine forty-five.
BARMAN: Sold your last then, did you?
MAN: Yes, my last 'Evening News' it was. Went about twenty to ten.
Pause.
BARMAN: 'Evening News', was it?
MAN: Yes.

Pause.
Sometimes it's the 'Star' is the last to go.
BARMAN: Ah!
MAN: Or the . . . whatsisname.
BARMAN: 'Standard'.
MAN: Yes.
Pause.
All I had left tonight was the 'Evening News'.
Pause.
BARMAN: Then that went, did it?
MAN: Yes.
Pause.
Like a shot.
Pause.
BARMAN: You didn't have any left, eh?
MAN: No. Not after I sold that one.
Pause.
BARMAN: It was after that you must have come by here then, was it?
MAN: Yes, I come by here after that, see, after I packed up.
BARMAN: You didn't stop here though, did you?
MAN: When?
BARMAN: I mean, you didn't stop here and have a cup of tea then, did you?
MAN: What, about ten?
BARMAN: Yes.
MAN: No, I went up to Victoria.
BARMAN: No, I thought I didn't see you.
MAN: I had to go up to Victoria.
Pause.
BARMAN: Yes, trade was very brisk here about then.
Pause.
MAN: I went to see if I could get hold of George.
BARMAN: Who?
MAN: George.
Pause.
BARMAN: George who?
MAN: George . . . whatsisname.
BARMAN: Oh!
Pause.
Did you get hold of him?
MAN: No. No, I couldn't get hold of him. I couldn't locate him.
BARMAN: He's not about much now, is he?
Pause.
MAN: When did you last see him then?
BARMAN: Oh, I haven't seen him for years.
MAN: No, nor me.
Pause.
BARMAN: Used to suffer very bad from arthritis.
MAN: Arthritis?
BARMAN: Yes.
MAN: He never suffered from arthritis.
BARMAN: Suffered very bad.
Pause.
MAN: Not when I knew him.
Pause.
BARMAN: I think he must have left the area.
Pause.
MAN: Yes, it was the 'Evening News' was the last to go tonight.

BARMAN: Not always the last though, is it, though?
MAN: No. Oh no. I mean sometimes it's the 'News'. Other times it's one of the others. No way of telling beforehand. Until you've got your last one left, of course. Then you can tell which one it's going to be.
BARMAN: Yes.
Pause.
MAN: Oh yes.
Pause.
I think he must have left the area.

Last To Go:
Harold Pinter

Comment

This sketch shows Harold Pinter's skill in creating a dialogue that seems hauntingly real and familiar: the pauses as the two characters stumble through their conversation, the trivial details mentioned, and the way in which the subject of conversation changes and comes back. Dialogue similar to this can be heard every day.

Humour presents itself in the form of obvious statements: there is no way of telling which paper will be last, until there is only one left. But in spite of some humour, there remains an air of sadness; the characters cannot, or will not, reveal too much of themselves to each other. Their humdrum lives will continue.

In the dullness of their conversation there seem to be the seeds of excitement, perhaps an approaching argument, when the MAN declares that George 'never suffered from arthritis'. But the climax is short-lived, as they return to their 'safe' theme.

Activities

– Listen to a snatch or two of conversation – at a bus stop, disco, shop, for example – and work it into a short sketch.
– With the help of a friend, make a recording of *Last To Go*. What sound effects would you need? Think very carefully about the length of the many pauses. If you pause for too long the tension is lost; the timing of such pauses is crucial and needs practice.
– Write a short story centred on a coffee stall in a city. Do not restrict it to the characters in the sketch.
– Harold Pinter has written several sketches, as well as full-length plays. Try reading some, though they were, of course, meant for performance; there is plenty of scope for performance by a school drama club.

Nuts and Bolts

Write brief notes – only three or four **instructions** – on how to set out a play. You will need to mention stage directions, characters and arrangement of speeches.

Note the use of full stops. What are three **dots** (. . .) for?

The names of newspapers are given with quotation marks; it is more usual to print them in *italics*.

What are the **apostrophes** for in: didn't, couldn't, he's and you've? What would the full forms of the words be?

Unit 14

The furnaces of the earth

When champagne is uncorked, the gas dissolved in the wine suddenly expands and fizz spouts from the bottle. Similarly, a crack in rocks caused by pressure beneath can produce spouts of glowing lava-fizz. These fountains may play for several days before the pressure below is relieved and they fall.

The titanic forces that built the Himalayas and all the other mountains on earth proceed so slowly that they are normally invisible to our eyes. But occasionally they burst into the most dramatic displays of force that the world can show. The earth begins to shake and the land explodes.

If the lava that erupts from the ground is basalt, black and heavy, then the area may have been continuously active for many centuries. Iceland is just such a place. Almost every year there is a volcanic activity of some kind. Molten rock spills out from huge cracks that run right across the island. Often it is an ugly tide of hot basalt boulders that advances over the land in a creeping unstoppable flood. It creaks as the rocks cool and crack. It rattles as lumps tumble from its front edge. Sometimes the basalt is more liquid. Then a fountain of fire, orange red at the sides, piercing yellow at its centre, may spout 50 metres into the air with a sustained roar, like a gigantic jet engine. Molten basalt splashes around the vent. Lava froth is thrown high above the main plume where the howling wind catches it, cools it and blows it away to coat distant rocks with layers of grey prickly grit. If you approach upwind, much of the heat as well as the ash is blown away from you, so that you can stand within 50 metres of the vent without scorching your face, though when the wind veers, ash will begin to fall around you and large red-hot lumps land with a thud and sizzle in the snow nearby. You must then either keep a sharp eye out for flying boulders or run for it.

Floods of cooling black lava stretch all around the vent. Walking over the corded, blistered surface, you can see in the cracks that, only a few inches beneath, it is still red hot. Here and there, gas within the lava has formed an immense bubble, the roof of which is so thin that it can easily collapse beneath your foot with a splintering crash. If, as well as such alarms, you also find yourself fighting for breath because of unseen, unsmelt poisonous gas, you will be wise to go no further. But you may now be close enough to see the most awesome sight of all – a lava river. The liquid rock surges up from the vent with such force that it forms a trembling dome. From there it gushes in a torrent, 20 metres across maybe, and streams down the slope at an astonishing speed, sometimes as much as 100 kilometres an hour. As night falls, this extraordinary scarlet river illuminates everything around it a baleful red. Its incandescent surface spurts bubbles of gas and the air above it trembles with the heat. Within a few hundred yards of its source, the edges of the flow have cooled sufficiently to solidify, so now the scarlet river runs between banks of black rock. Farther down still, the surface of the flow begins to skin over. But beneath this solid roof the lava surges on and will continue to do so for several miles more, for not only is basaltic lava extremely liquid in character, but the walls and ceiling of solid rock that now surround it act as insulators, keeping in the heat and preventing it from congealing. When, after days or weeks, the supply of lava from the vent stops, the river continues to flow downwards until the tunnel is drained, leaving behind it a great winding cavern. These lava tubes, as they are called, may be as high as 10 metres and run for several kilometres up the core of a lava flow.

The hard rocky shell of the earth is cracked into seven huge pieces and several smaller ones. The junctions between them are marked by lines of volcanoes and shaken by earthquakes, for all these plates are in continuous motion relative to one another. Those that carry continents, such as the American, African and Eurasian plates, are moving at a rate of about 2.5 centimetres a year. Those that lie beneath the Pacific are travelling five or six times faster.

The Living Planet:
David Attenborough

In January, 1973, the inhabitants of the Westmann Islands, a cluster of islands off the southern coast of Iceland, were woken up at about two o'clock in the morning:

The town was tranquil, but just to the east of it the ground began to quiver slightly. Pebbles were thrown up in the air, as if they had been lying on a taut skin which someone had struck lightly. Then the surface of the land appeared to swell up, and soon it began to crack. It was as if a sharp knife were being drawn over the flesh of the earth and blood were beginning to spurt. Only, it was not blood; it was fire and embers. In a matter of minutes, nearly a mile-long fissure opened, running from north-north-east to south-south-west. Lava immediately began to well out of it, and glowing cinders squirted high into the air. The fissure consisted of dozens of eye-like small craters, forming a continuous row of fire east of the town. At the north-north-eastern end of it, which reached all the way down to the sea, the fire was very close to the easternmost houses. From there, the crack ran south-south-westward, directly across the eastern part of the island, reaching the sea at that end also. Witnesses do not agree exactly when the eruption began, but most maintain it was at 1.55 a.m. The clock on the Town Hall stopped at that time, and it has not been going since.

Volcano – Ordeal by Fire in Iceland's Westmann Islands: Arni Gunnarsson

Comment

David Attenborough explains with enthusiasm a complex geological process; we can sense, through the vigorous language he uses, his understanding and experience of volcanoes. Through his books and films he has brought to many people knowledge of and consideration for the planet on which we live.

The second piece, concerning the start of the eruption in the Westmann Islands, presents a personal account in a calm way. It is calm because the Icelanders have had plenty of opportunity to come to terms with volcanic eruptions.

Activities

– Write a fifty-word news flash for radio, reporting the eruption in the Westmann Islands.
– Imagine you have ten minutes to leave your home because volcanic lava is approaching. List the things you would do and what you would take with you.
– Having read David Attenborough's article, summarize its contents and explain to someone else what it says.
– Look these words up in your dictionary, and then see how each one is used in the passage: veer, baleful, incandescent, congeal.
– What is a seismologist?
– Find out about Vesuvius, Etna, Surtsey and Hekla.
– Design a postage stamp commemorating a volcanic eruption.
– Who were the Titans and Vulcan?

Nuts and Bolts

Look at the second half of the third paragraph, and find words which appeal to the **senses** of sight, sound, touch and feeling.

After the details of date and time and place, the second piece gives us the impression made on the inhabitants at the time, and brings in two **similes** to help. Write down the first six words of each simile.

'Volcanoes' reminds us of the **plurals** of other words ending in **o**. 'Volcanoes' has been in the language for at least three hundred years; so have: hero, cargo, potato and tomato, and they all have plurals in **-oes**. More recent words have **-os**: photos, radios, dynamos, studios. What is the plural of 'disco'?

Unit 15

The cat sat on the mat

If we change the title of this unit from 'The cat sat on the mat' to 'The cat sat on the dog's mat', you will see that the second title has possibilities for making up a short story that the first lacks. All stories must have a point to make, though not necessarily of the possible conflict that 'The cat sat on the dog's mat' suggests.

Let's look at a short story, set in war-time:

The station was crowded with women and children all clutching as much luggage as they could, and intent on leaving the city. A couple of teenagers, laughing and giggling, occupied a compartment with a middle-aged woman, slumped down in her seat muttering from time to time, 'One, two, three,' in a most distracted manner. These often repeated words caused evident amusement to the teenagers, and they began to make insulting comments about her.

'One, two, three,' she continued.

After a while a fourth occupant, a weary-faced man, leant forward and said, in a soft voice, 'Excuse me, young friends, but I think I ought to tell you that this lady is my wife. We have lost our three sons, all soldiers, in the war. I'm on my way to take my wife to a special home.'

The compartment went very quiet.

What is the point of this story? If you think for a moment you will probably say that we should be careful not to judge or ridicule people. Acquainted with the reason for the woman's muttering and her obvious suffering, the teenagers are stunned into silence. There is the briefest of descriptions, just enough to fix the scene for us: railway station, women and children, luggage. The writer tells us more by implication; by specifying women and children he makes us realize that there are few men about – they are away at the battle-front. We read between the lines.

Is it long enough to be a short story? Some short stories seem to go on for pages while others, like this, only last a paragraph or two. It is impossible to give a hard and fast rule about such matters, though a helpful way of considering it may be to say that a short story is as long as it needs to be. This may sound a little cryptic (what does that word mean?), but it makes sense: in writing a story you should make the point as effectively and economically as possible – and then stop.

The novelist can take her time. She can spread herself out, so to speak, having several locations and plenty of characters. But the writer of the short story needs to prune away everything but the essentials. We need just a minimum of description to set the scene. Remember that with so much television, so many books and magazines full of photographs, and with so many people travelling far more than was the case even thirty years ago, readers can bring much experience of their own to the story.

Instead of description, the writer needs to concentrate on characters and particularly on what the characters say. Listen carefully to conversation going on about you, whether in a supermarket queue, at a bus-stop, or on the beach. If you enjoy writing stories, keep a note-book to jot down bits of conversation that you hear (though probably best not in front of the speakers!). Many ideas can start in this way and it will be good training for you in achieving natural-sounding dialogue.

Your characters will not only speak, they will do things, they will act. And the writer can show the characters' feelings most effectively by the way they act and respond. The writer of the story above had no need to say that the teenagers were shocked at the woman's plight and were sorry they had made fun of her. Their silence after their laughing, giggling, commenting, is sufficient. In fact, if the writer had said how shocked they were, there would not have been the same impact.

Bearing these points in mind, read this story by Frank Sargeson:

Boy

For my birthday my father promised me a box of paints.

'If he behaves himself,' my mother said.

I began counting the days, and at the rate they went I didn't see how I'd reach my birthday this side of being an old man.

With a week to go I reckoned it was time to remind my father about the paints just in case he'd forgotten. But it turned out I didn't remind him because that afternoon after school I broke the window of the shed in our back-yard. It wasn't the first time either, though always an accident of course.

But the last time was almost too long ago to remember. That's how it seemed to me anyhow, though I did sort of somehow remember clearly enough that I'd been promised a thrashing the next time it happened. So I got quite a surprise when all my father did was to promise me a thrashing if it happened again.

It had me properly worried. Things being what they were I didn't feel like reminding my father about the box of paints, but I thought if he could forget one promise he could just as easily forget another.

At breakfast on the morning of my birthday, mother gave me six new handkerchiefs. And father told me that he'd bring the box of paints when he came home from work that evening.

Well, that afternoon after school I was out in the back-yard with my shanghai, and when I took a shot at a thrush that came and sat on our gooseberry bush you can guess what happened. My hand slipped of course.

Mother heard the noise and came to the kitchen door. 'You know what your father said,' she said, and went inside again.

When my father came home I was in my room lying on my bed. I heard him put his bike away in the shed and then I could hear him and mother talking in the kitchen. And then mother called out for me to come to dinner.

I went, and my father was sitting in his place taking a look at the paper before he carved the meat. I sat down and we had dinner and I never said a word and father and mother never talked much either. And I could see the box of paints wrapped in brown paper lying on the top of the sewing machine.

When he'd finished his dinner my father took out his pipe and pointed.

'Your paints are over there,' he said.

'First you can help me with the dishes,' my mother said.

But I dropped the tea-towel when I saw my father light a candle and go out to put another piece of glass in the window.

'I'll hold the candle, father,' I said. 'And here's the putty-knife, father,' I said.

I helped him a lot I can tell you. I helped him until he growled at me for helping him and told me to go and help my mother instead.

Later on that evening I painted a thrush in mid-air with a most painful look on its face and half its feathers flying. I told my father and mother it was because I'd landed it with my shanghai.

Neither of them seemed to think much of my painting.

'It's half an hour past your bedtime,' my mother said.

I felt like telling her it was only twenty-five minutes, but I somehow thought with my father there I'd better not.

But it was only the next day that my father heard me answering my mother back, and oh gee if he didn't lay it on.

Collected Stories:
Frank Sargeson

Activities

– Many of the best stories are sparked off by a chance remark, a particular scene, or a character. *Boy* sounds as if it has been prompted by personal experience – either of the writer or of someone known to him. Here are some possible ideas or starting-points for stories:

- The wind blew the leaves and dust along the city street.
- One look from my mother was enough.
- 'It was most welcome, I can assure you,' said the English teacher.
- The last day of the holidays. . . .
- A piece of linen was sufficient. . . .
- I hadn't noticed that the fruit bowl had been moved.
- On closing the book I realized that this was only the start.
- I was sure I would see him again.

– Reading short stories by established authors is an excellent way of learning the craft of writing them yourself. Here are half a dozen to try:
The Luncheon: Somerset Maugham; *The Wave*: Liam O'Flaherty; *The Signalman*: Charles Dickens; *Eveline*: James Joyce; *Strike Pay*: D.H. Lawrence; *The Rain Horse*: Ted Hughes.

Unit 16

A father no more

Miyax, a beautiful Eskimo girl, lost her mother as a child, and then her father was reported drowned. At thirteen she became the girl wife of a stupid brute. So with food and sleeping kit she set out across barren land to Point Hope, en route for San Francisco, where a friend lived. But she lost her way, ran out of food, and survived by making friends – in a way taught by her father – with Amaroq the leader of a wolf pack. With a golden plover, Tornait, which had been blown off course, she reached a village where she had been told her father still lived. They meet:

'Yes,' he whispered. 'Yes, you are she. You are beautiful like your mother.' He opened his arms. She ran into them and for a long time he held her tightly.

'When they sent you to school,' he said softly, 'Nunivak was too much to bear. I left and began a new life. Last year when at last I was rich I went back to get you. You were gone.' His fingers touched her hair and he hugged her once more.

The door opened and the woman came in. 'Who have we here?' she asked in English.

Miyax saw that her face was pale and her hair was reddish gold. A chill spread over her. What had Kapugen done? What had happened to him that he would marry a gussak? What was his new life?

Kapugen and his woman talked – she loudly, Kapugen quietly. Miyax's eyes went round the room again. This time she saw not just the furs and the kayak, but electric lamps, a radio-phonograph, cotton curtains and, through the door to the annexe, the edge of an electric stove, a coffee pot, and china dishes. There were bookshelves and a framed picture on the wall of some American country garden. Then she saw a helmet and goggles on a chair. Miyax stared at them until Kapugen noticed her.

'Aw, that,' he said. 'I now own an aeroplane, Miyax. It's the only way to hunt today. The seals are scarce and the whales are almost gone; but sportsmen can still hunt from planes.'

Miyax heard no more. It could not be, it could not be. She would not let it be. She instantly buried what she was thinking in the shadows of her mind.

'Miyax,' the wife said in bad Upick, 'I teach in the school here. We shall enrol you tomorrow. You can learn to read and write English. It's very difficult to live even in this Eskimo town without knowing English.'

Miyax looked at Kapugen. 'I am on my way to San Francisco,' she said softly in Upick. 'The gussaks in Wainwright have arranged transportation for me. I shall go tomorrow.'

A telephone rang. Kapugen answered it and jotted down a note.

'I'll be right back,' he said to Miyax. 'I'll be right back. Then we'll talk.' He hugged her. Miyax stiffened and looked at the helmet.

'Ellen, fix her some food,' he called as he put on his coat, a long American-made Arctic field jacket. He zipped it with a flourish and went out of the door. Ellen went into the kitchen and Miyax was alone.

Slowly she picked up Tornait, put on her sealskin parka, and placed the little bird in her hood. Then she snapped on the radio, and as it crackled, whined, and picked up music, she opened the door and softly closed it behind her. Kapugen, after all, was dead to her.

On the second bench of the river above town she found her tent and pack, threw them onto her sled and, bending forward, hauled on it. She walked on up the river towards her house. She was an Eskimo, and as an Eskimo she must live. She would build snowhouses in winter, a sod house in summer. She would carve and sew and trap. And someday there would be a boy like herself. They would raise children, who would live with the rhythm of the beasts and the land.

'The seals are scarce and the whales are almost gone,' she heard Kapugen say. 'When are you coming to live with us in San Francisco?' called Amy.

Miyax walked backwards, watching the river valley. When the last light of Kangik disappeared, the stars lit the snow and the cold deepened far below zero. The ice thundered and boomed, roaring like drumbeats across the Arctic.

Tornait peeped. Miyax turned her head, touched him with her chin, and felt his limpness. She stopped walking and lifted him into the cold.

'Tornait. What is wrong with you? Are you sick?' Swiftly opening her pack, she took out some meat, chewed it to thaw it, and gave it to the bird. He refused to eat. She put him inside her parka and pitched her tent out of the wind. When she had banked it with snow, she lit a small fire. The tent glowed, then warmed. Tornait lay in her hands, his head on her fingers; he peeped softly and closed his eyes.

Many hours later she buried him in the snow. The totem of Amaroq was in her pocket. Her fingers ran over it but she did not take it out. She sang to the spirit of Amaroq in her best English:

The seals are scarce and the whales are almost
gone.
The spirits of the animals are passing away.
Amaroq, Amaroq, you are my adopted father.
My feet dance because of you.
My eyes see because of you.
My mind thinks because of you. And it thinks, on
this thundering night,

That the hour of the wolf and the Eskimo is over.

Julie of the Wolves:
Jean Craighead George

Comment

A gussak is a non-Eskimo; a kayak (one was in the roof of Kapugen's house) is a light canoe; the totem was a little figure of a wolf carved by Miyax; the house she went back to was built by herself. 'She had her needles, her knife, her sled and her tent, and the world of her ancestors. And she liked the simplicity of that world. It was easy to understand. Out here she understood how she fitted into the scheme of the moon and stars and the constant rise and fall of life on the earth.' The Eskimos had lived for generations in a hostile climate by living off the land, but not exploiting it, by co-operating with nature instead of destroying it, as her father was now doing. It was the sight of the helmet that finally turned her against her father, because she had seen Amaroq shot down from an aircraft, not long after he had saved her life by warning off a grizzly bear.

Activities

– Do you think Miyax was right to leave in the manner she did? Or would it have been better to have talked the matter over with her father? Jot down your thoughts.

– What do you think were Kapugen's thoughts, when he discovered that Miyax had disappeared?

– List the different attitudes towards Eskimo life of Miyax and Kapugen.

– Find out about modern Eskimo life. You will need an up-to-date encyclopaedia or geography or travel book. Ask your librarian if you have difficulty in finding something appropriate.

– Read the book (a moving story of survival in the frozen plains of Alaska) from which this extract has been taken. Another book worth reading is the true account by Olive Murray Chapman of her journey before the Second World War, *Across Lapland*.

– Write a piece entitled 'The Difficult Journey'. You can make it fact or fiction.

Nuts and Bolts

Miyax stares at the helmet, and a little later looks at it again, so clearly it means something to her. Think what it stands for, to her; and then note that the helmet is a **symbol**.

'Dishes' reminds us that the **plurals** of hissing words, like 'crash' and 'bus' and 'scratch', are formed by adding **-es**, to reproduce their sound when spoken aloud.

Most words ending in **f** have their plural in **-ves**, like 'knives' and 'thieves', but a few like 'chiefs' and 'roofs' keep their **f**. Some can go either way: handkerchief, hoof, staff. Remember 'chiefs' and 'roofs' firmly, and you won't go far wrong.

Unit 17

Hunted by wolves

This is the true story of an adventure that happened during the great Gold Rush of 1899 to Alaska. There were two kinds of wolf in the North-west: small grey wolves hunting in packs, which would only attack a man if he were helpless, and timber wolves. The latter were big enough and strong enough to pull down a moose; they hunted in couples and were very cunning. Here Mitchell tells Angus Graham of his first encounter with timber wolves:

I had gone off prospecting by myself, and made a little camp for the night a few miles down-stream from Bear Run Creek. Before I turned in for the night, I hung up my gold-pan on a bush – McQuaide had told me that the tinkling of a pan against the branches of a bush would keep me safe against wild animals anywhere. But the next morning, when I went down to the river to fill my billycan, I was horrified to see a dog's tracks that were bigger than my fist. If it was a dog I figured it was too big, and if it was a wolf that wasn't healthy either, so I turned back to my tent, made my breakfast, packed up and got started. But just as I was leaving I saw two prick ears showing up over a bush – it was a wolf all right. The brute shrank out of sight as I looked, but when I moved on it followed me, keeping under cover, and presently I found that there were two of them, working the hunt together.

Every now and then one of them showed itself in the open and I had a shot at it, but they were as quick as the devil – you'd think they saw the flash and dodged the bullet almost – and I never touched them once. After I'd had several cracks I happened to look at my belt, and I'd got only two more rounds left! I'd come out with a heavy pack and had cut down my ammunition to six or eight rounds to save weight. 'God,' I said, 'no more shooting, Mitchell, you keep those rounds for yourself': if they'd got me, I tell you I wasn't going to be torn to pieces alive!

As I went on without firing the wolves gradually realised that there was no danger, and they got more and more cheeky, keeping closer and closer to me and calling to each other to check up on my movements. They didn't often show themselves out and out, and must have bellied across the open spots like an Indian, but there were always the pointed ears showing over a boulder or a bush, or a flash of grey fur between tree-trunks, and the feeling that you were being watched.

The worst thing of all was the eyes in the fire-light after dark. I got no sleep that night, as I was keeping up the fire the whole time, and every now and then those eyes would draw up until I had to throw a burning stick at them. All the next day the same thing went on, and no rest again the next night – fire-light, and eyes, and I tell you I was getting pretty rattled. Then on the morning of the third day I saw they'd get me sure if this thing went on, and I thought it was about time to build a raft and go wherever it would take me. So I got hold of some driftwood, strapped it together with my packstraps and tump-line, and launched myself – and I – well had to use up one of my two last shots on them as I was pushing off. They followed the raft down along the sands, but eventually it fetched up on the other side of the river, and I got away. Of course the Indians said afterwards that it was my own fault for going out alone.

After he had finished this story Mitchell suddenly bent forward and banged the arm of his chair. 'Graham,' he said, 'there are no words in the English language that I can use to convey to you the horror of feeling yourself a hunted animal. I shall never forget it – the eyes in the darkness, and the fear of something that *lurks*. I have been familiar with wolves for years after those days, but I've never got used to the sound of their howling, which is enough to make anyone shudder. Yet those devils that hunted me, they didn't howl – they ran a still-hunt, and that was almost worse in a way. You felt them always pressing on you, always just behind you, always just round that boulder, always watching for the moment when you would stumble or nod asleep – and then leap in!

The Golden Grindstone:
Angus Graham

Old wolf

Lopes on purpose, padding the snow
Of the soft-brown winterlocked landscape,
Under the loaded branches in the hush of the
  forests.
Stops for its own reasons, shapeless
In the white shadows that have
Stopped breathing.
The prints run into the dark and
The stars wheel, circling the silence.

James Taylor

Music hath charms

A pleasant tale I heard of a soldier in Ireland, who having got his passport to go for England, as he passed through the wood with his knapsack on his back, being weary, he sat down under a tree. He opened his knapsack, and fell to some victuals he had; but on a sudden he was surprised by two or three wolves. As they came towards him, he threw them scraps of bread and cheese till all was gone. Then the wolves making a nearer approach to him he knew not what shift to make. But he took up a pair of bagpipes which he had, and as soon as he began to play, the wolves all ran away as if they had been scared out of their wits.

Whereupon the soldier said, 'A pox take you all, if I had known you loved music so well you should have had it before dinner.'

James Howell, 1594–1666

Comment

The man Mitchell who told Angus Graham about his escape broke a leg during the Gold Rush, and was restored to health by the care and medicine of the Red Indians who looked after him. It is a fascinating story, full of exciting events. In the piece above the suspense builds up from the point at which Mitchell sees the big tracks; we feel what it is like to be watched, and how narrowly he escaped.

Activities

– Stories often have a point at which events take a decisive turn: the climax. Can you find one in Mitchell's adventure?
– Imagine a newspaper is running a daily series entitled *Brave People*. The editor wants true stories, about 200 words long. You decide to write about Mitchell.
– Find out as much as you can about the Gold Rush and write a piece of historical fiction based on your research.
– Do you know of anyone who has been in a position of great danger? If so, chat to him or her about the occasion. Is there enough to start you thinking up a short story?
– Did you read the novels and story by Jack London, that we recommended in Unit 16 of Volume 1? If not, you may like to do so now.

Nuts and Bolts

Look at the final paragraph of the extract from *The Golden Grindstone*, and notice the help you get in reading it aloud from **dashes**, ***italics*** and an **exclamation mark**. What word would you stress in reading the last few lines aloud?

Many English words can be used as a **noun**, an **adjective** or a **verb**; and you can often make up a verb from a noun to suit your needs. For example: the train **snaked** across the landscape. (You are not allowed to do this in French.) Find the word used to describe the way the wolves moved when there was no cover.

Adverbs can be made from **adjectives** ending in **l** by adding **-ly** – gradual, gradually. Find another example in the last paragraph but one.

What would you tell a learner to note about: branches, horrified, strapped? Note the 'eight' family and add a few of its relatives.

Unit 18

The night the bed fell

Father has gone to bed in the attic to be alone with his thoughts, but Mother is afraid that the headboard of the wobbly old bed will fall and kill him. Briggs is a nervous cousin, obsessed with the idea that he might stop breathing in the night and die. So he keeps a glass of spirits of camphor nearby to revive him:

In the front room upstairs (just under father's attic bedroom) were my mother and my brother Herman, who sometimes sang in his sleep, usually 'Marching Through Georgia' or 'Onward Christian Soldiers'. Briggs and myself were in a room adjoining this one. My brother Roy was in a room across the hall from ours. Our bull terrier, Rex, slept in the hall.

My bed was an army cot, one of those affairs which are made wide enough to sleep on comfortably only by putting up, flat with the middle section, the two sides which ordinarily hang down like the sideboards of a drop-leaf table. When these sides are up, it is perilous to roll too far towards the edge, for then the cot is likely to tip completely over, bringing the whole bed down on top of one, with a tremendous banging crash. This, in fact, is precisely what happened, about two o'clock in the morning. (It was my mother who, in recalling the scene later, first referred to it as 'the night the bed fell on your father.')

Always a deep sleeper, slow to arouse, I was at first unconscious of what happened when the iron cot rolled me onto the floor and toppled over on me. It left me still warmly bundled up and unhurt, for the bed rested above me like a canopy. Hence I did not wake up, only reached the edge of consciousness and went back. The racket, however, instantly awakened my mother, in the next room, who came to the immediate conclusion that her worst dread was realised: the big wooden bed upstairs had fallen on father. She therefore screamed, 'Let's go to your poor father!' It was this shout, rather than the noise of my cot falling, that awakened Herman, in the same room with her. He thought that mother had become, for no apparent reason, hysterical. 'You're all right, Mamma!' he shouted, trying to calm her. They exchanged shout for shout for perhaps ten seconds. 'Let's go to your poor father!' and 'You're all right!' That woke up Briggs. By this time I was conscious of what was going on, in a vague way, but did not yet realise that I was under the bed instead of on it. Briggs, awakening in the midst of loud shouts of fear and apprehension, came to the quick conclusion that he was suffocating and that we were all trying to 'bring him out'. With a low moan, he grasped the glass of camphor at the head of his bed and instead of sniffing it poured it over himself. The room reeked of camphor. 'Ugf, ahfg,' choked Briggs, like a drowning man, for he had almost succeeded in stopping his breath under the deluge of pungent spirits. He leaped out of bed and groped toward the open window, but he came up against one that was closed. With his hand he beat out the glass, and I could hear it crash and tinkle on the alleyway below. It was at this juncture that I, in trying to get up, had the uncanny sensation of feeling my bed above me! Foggy with sleep, I now suspected, in my turn, that the whole uproar was being made in a frantic endeavour to extricate me from what must be an unheard of and perilous situation. 'Get me out of this!' I bawled. 'Get me out!' I think I had the nightmarish belief that I was entombed in a mine. 'Gugh,' gasped Briggs, floundering in his camphor.

By this time my mother, still shouting, pursued by Herman, still shouting, was trying to open the door to the attic, in order to go up and get my father's body out of the wreckage. The door was stuck, however, and wouldn't yield. Her frantic pulls on it only added to the general banging and confusion. Roy and the dog were now up, the one shouting questions, the other barking.

Father, farthest away and soundest sleeper of all, had by this time been awakened by the battering on the attic door. He decided that the house was on fire. 'I'm coming, I'm coming!' he wailed in a slow, sleepy voice – it took him many minutes to regain full consciousness. My mother, still believing he was caught under the bed, detected in his 'I'm coming!' the resigned note of one who is preparing to meet his Maker. 'He's dying!' she shouted.

'I'm all right!' Briggs yelled to reassure her. He still believed that it was his own closeness to death that was worrying mother. I found at last the light switch in my room, and Briggs and I joined the others in the attic. The dog, who never did like Briggs, jumped for him – assuming that he was the culprit in whatever was going on – and Roy had to throw Rex and hold him. We could hear father crawling out of bed upstairs. Roy pulled the attic door open, with a mighty jerk, and father came down the stairs, sleepy and irritable but safe and sound. My mother began to weep when she saw him. Rex began to howl. 'What in the name of God is going on here?' asked father.

The situation was finally put together like a gigantic jig-saw puzzle. Father caught a cold from prowling around in his bare feet but there were no other bad results. 'I'm glad,' said mother, who always looked on the bright side of things, 'that your grandfather wasn't here.'

My Life and Hard Times:
James Thurber

Comment

In his Preface Thurber records that he was born in Parsons Avenue, Columbus, Ohio. 'Once his mother, walking past the place with an old lady from Fostoria, said to her, "My son James was born in that house," to which the old lady, who was extremely deaf, replied, "Why, on the Tuesday morning train, unless my sister gets worse." My mother let it go at that.'

He makes everyone funny, including himself, but his humour is always kindly, never cruel. He ends his Preface with best wishes to his readers for a happy new world.

Activities

– Invent a short story about a similar family in which something happens to cause complete confusion and cross-purposes.
– Describe the oddest dream you have ever had.
– Dip into *The Thurber Carnival* or any other books by Thurber.
– Compose the diary entry that Briggs might have written about the night the bed fell.
– From this and the other pieces you have read by James Thurber (Unit 16, 'Rex', in Volume 1; Unit 2, 'Muggs', in this volume) you will have gained a fair idea of the Thurber family. Talk to parents and friends about them.
– If you are not quite sure of them, use your dictionary to get the meanings of these words clear: hysterical, apprehension, pungent, juncture, extricate.

Nuts and Bolts

In the second paragraph of the extract you will see the **adverb** 'only'. It is rightly placed; and this is important with a word that gives different meanings according to its **position**:

Only Sue fed the cat (Sue and no one else).
Sue **only** fed the cat (she didn't do anything else).
Sue fed **only** the cat (she didn't feed anything else).

Always get an adverb as near as you can to the word it is meant to assist.

Think of two other words in which, like 'dread' in this piece, **ea** sounds like 'e'.

Unit 19

Faith and Henry

Place: Lancashire
The camera moves up towards the entrance of a school. The doors open to let out a rush of children. The camera selects a girl of about sixteen as she comes through the doors. She stands for a moment on the steps leading down from the doors. She looks round at the trees and the sky, and smiles as she takes a deep breath of fresh air. Then she suddenly jumps down the few steps to the drive. A boy of about seventeen has come out of the doors behind her and, as she jumps, he gives a little cheer. He is a tall fellow with a cheery face. She turns and looks at him and smiles.
HENRY: All set for the Olympics?
She laughs and he jumps down to her. They walk down the path side by side not speaking. Occasionally their eyes meet. They reach the gate to the street and turn in the same direction. Other children jostle against them. We watch them walking to the bus stop.
FAITH: Catching the bus?
HENRY: Not today. I'm buying cheese.
FAITH: Catching mice then?
HENRY: Not today, cheeky. I always buy cheese on a Thursday.
FAITH: Why?
HENRY: It's fresh.
They stare around rather self-consciously. Quite a crowd of children are at the stop now, making a din. There are boys shoving and pushing. Henry looks down and shouts.
HENRY: Shut up!
The crowd becomes orderly. He glances down at the girl. Her look holds the correct admiration.
FAITH: You used to go home the other way.
HENRY: We moved.
FAITH: To the council houses?
HENRY: Yes.
FAITH: Quite nice, aren't they?
HENRY: They're all right.
FAITH: Nice and modern.
HENRY: Mother's got a good name for them.
FAITH: Yeh?

HENRY: Luxury boxes.
She laughs. The bus appears.
HENRY: Faith–
FAITH: How do you know my name?
HENRY: Made it my business.
FAITH: Mr Spy.
HENRY: Tell you what–don't get on the bus.
FAITH: I'm going home.
HENRY: Come with me.
FAITH: And buy cheese.
HENRY: *You* don't need to buy cheese.
FAITH: I'm going home.
HENRY: All right.
He shrugs, turns on his heel and leaves her as the bus draws up. She waits for the bus to stop and looks over her shoulder at him walking off. She suddenly leaves the bus and runs after him. Some lads whistle after her. She reaches Henry and he looks down at her startled.
HENRY: What's this?
FAITH: I fancied a bit of cheese.
She giggles and his face lights up. They walk off briskly.

A GROCERY SHOP
The boy and girl enter a large old-fashioned shop. There is a cavernous coolness about the interior of it. They look at each other and she looks away.
FAITH: Where's the cheese?
HENRY: Follow your nose.
FAITH: Eh?
He turns her round and pushes her towards the cheese counter. She holds her nose.
FAITH: How right you are!
There is a wonderful display of cheeses, in pride of place two great Lancashire cheeses. The offending smell comes from a rich gorgonzola. There is a small man behind the counter. He is like a beautifully scrubbed pink mouse. He notes Faith's pinched nose, and lays his hand lovingly on the gorgonzola.

MR FORSHAW: A lovely cheese that.
FAITH (*through her nose*): It stinks.
MR FORSHAW (*his accent rich and broad*): A lovely cheese – nicely ripe.
FAITH: It's mouldy.
The man looks at her with mild distress.
MR FORSHAW: Lass – you know nowt about cheese.
FAITH: I don't want to know anything about that one.
MR FORSHAW: This – (*He regards the cheese as if it were a jewel*) is a perfect gorgonzola. Trouble has been taken with that cheese, lass – great care and trouble – and there are folks eat nowt else.
Faith would like to giggle, but the little man is too serious, and Henry is obviously on his side. The man looks enquiringly at Henry.
HENRY: The usual please, Mr Forshaw.
He beams at Henry and starts to cut a large piece of gorgonzola. Faith watches – fascinated.
FAITH: Who eats that in your house?
HENRY: Our dad eats it – after his dinner.
MR FORSHAW: Henry's dad knows cheese. (*He wraps up the cheese.*) Well then, Henry?
HENRY: And the usual Lancashire, Mr Forshaw.
MR FORSHAW: One pound and a half of Lancashire cheese.
FAITH: How much?
HENRY: Pound and a half.
FAITH: Who eats all that, then?
She watches the big piece being cut.
MR FORSHAW: There are six in Henry's family – four boys and mum and dad and they all eat cheese.
Henry smiles down at Faith. He thrusts out his chest.
HENRY: Cheese is good for you – builds big bodies.
He says it like a TV advert. Faith laughs.
MR FORSHAW: D'you care for Lancashire cheese, lass?
FAITH: Never had it.
HENRY: Good lord.
MR FORSHAW: You don't know cheese. (*He pokes a lump at her.*) Try that.
(*He hands over the big parcel to Henry.*) Cheddar? (*Henry nods.*)
FAITH (*swallowing the cheese*): Not bad.
MR FORSHAW: Try it toasted, lass – Lancashire cheese toasted is a delicacy.
He is cutting the huge piece of Cheddar. Faith looks at it and then at Henry. Henry laughs outright. He takes the cheese, puts it in a string bag and pays for it.
HENRY: See you next week then, Mr Forshaw.
MR FORSHAW: My regards to your mother.
He bows his head in an almost regal gesture of goodbye. Faith and Henry walk off.

Faith and Henry:
Julia Jones

Comment

These are the opening scenes of a television play about the beginning of a friendship between a cheerful West Indian girl, Faith, who would like to fly aeroplanes, and Henry, a white boy.

Activities

– Continue the script for a couple of scenes or so.
– List the advantages and the disadvantages a film or television script has over a script for a stage play.
– You have to talk to the boy and girl chosen to play the parts of Faith and Henry. Summarize for them, very briefly, the characters.
– In what way is Faith like a yellowhammer? You may need to look at a book about birds to find out.
– Some shops, like the old-fashioned grocery shop in this script, seem to have much more character than others. Choose a favourite shop and try to capture its atmosphere in a poem.

Nuts and Bolts

Italics are used for two purposes in this unit. One is obvious; find the other, and say why the word is in italics.

The word 'wonderful' gives us no information about the display of cheeses, but it tells us much about the impression it makes on the beholder. Mr Forshaw applies to the gorgonzola another word, which is in the same class of **adjectives** as 'wonderful'. What is the word and what does it tell us?

When Henry says cheese 'builds big bodies' he is imitating a trick of advertising and newspaper headlines. What is it? Saying the words aloud will help.

Why do we invite you to notice the spelling of: occasionally, all right, fancied, beautifully, piece?

Unit 20

Kicking a ball about

The pleasures and pains of football are not new. Here is the view of Philip Stubbes, writing four hundred years ago:

For as concerning football playing, I protest unto you it may rather be called a friendly kind of fight, than a play or recreation; a bloody and murdering practice, than a fellowly sport or pastime. For doth not every one lie in wait for his adversary, seeking to overthrow him and to pitch him on his nose, though it be upon hard stones, in ditch or dale, in valley or hill, or what place soever it be he careth not, so he have him down. And he that can serve the most of this fashion, he is counted the only fellow, and who but he? So that by this means, sometimes their necks are broken, sometimes their backs, sometimes their legs, sometime their arms, sometime one part thrust out of joint, sometime another, sometime their noses gush out with blood, sometime their eyes start out, and sometimes hurt in one place, sometimes in another. But whosoever scapeth away the best goeth not scot-free, but is either sore wounded, and bruised, so as he dieth of it, or else scapeth very hardly. And no marvel, for they have sleights to meet one betwixt two, to dash him against the heart with their elbows, to hit him under the short ribs with their gripped fists, and with their knees to catch him upon the hip, and to pitch him on his neck, with an hundred such murdering devices. And hereof groweth envy, malice, rancour, choler, hatred, displeasure, enmity and what not else: and sometimes fighting, brawling, contention, quarrel picking, murder, homicide and great effusion of blood, as experience daily teacheth.

The Anatomie of Abuses

Nowadays, perhaps, this account seems to describe the antics of some spectators rather than the players.

The Russian writer, Yevgeny Yevtushenko, nearly became a footballer:

At night I wrote poetry and in the daytime I played football in backyards and on empty lots. I came home with torn trousers, battered shoes, and bleeding knees. The thud of the bouncing leather ball was, to me, the most intoxicating of all sounds.

To outflank the defences of the other side by feinting and dribbling and then to land a dead shot into the net past the helplessly spreadeagled goalkeeper, this seemed to me, as it still does now, somthing very like poetry.

Football taught me many things.

When I became a goalkeeper myself, I learnt to detect the slightest movement of the adversary's forwards and often to anticipate their feints. This was to be a help to me in my literary struggle.

People prophesied a brilliant career for me as a footballer.

Many of the boys I played with at school became professionals. On the rare occasions when I meet them now, I have a feeling that they envy me, and I catch myself out envying them.

Football is in many ways easier than poetry. If you score a goal you have concrete evidence: the ball is in the net. The fact, as they say, is indisputable. (The referee may after all disallow the goal but only exceptionally.) Whereas the likeliest thing to happen if you score a goal in poetry is for referees' whistles to shrill out to disallow it – and nothing can ever be proved. And very often an offside is declared a goal.

In general, in spite of all the intrigues and dirt that go with it, sport is a cleaner business than literature. There are times when I am very sorry I did not become a footballer.

I very nearly did.

After I had distinguished myself in a match – I kicked three penalties in succession – the coach of a famous team asked me to come and see him. All the other boys were green with envy.

But an event took place which determined my fate.

I had long been meaning to take my poems to the editor of *Soviet Sport* – it was about the only paper I had never sent them to.

I went after the match, in a washed-out blue T-shirt, tracksuit trousers, and torn plimsolls. I had in my hand a poem which contrasted the ways of American athletes with those of ours.

The editorial office of *Soviet Sport* was a big room in Dzerzhinsky Street, where through a fog of cigarette smoke and the clacking of typewriters, scratching pens and rustling of galleys, I could dimly make out several figures.

I asked timidly where the poetry section was. Somewhere in the fog a voice barked that there was no such section. But suddenly a hand, thrust out of the fog, fell on my shoulder and a voice asked:

'Poetry? Let's have a look . . .'

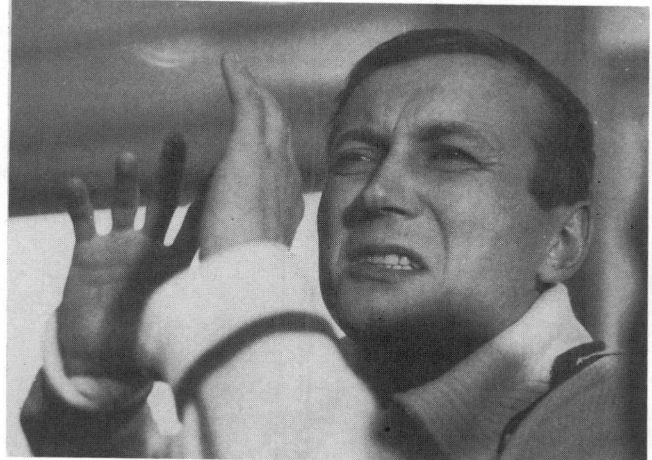

Yevgeny Yevtushenko

I trusted the hand and the voice at once. And I was right.

A Precocious Autobiography: Yevgeny Yevtushenko

Finally, a piece about one of the most famous footballers of all time, Stanley Matthews:

You get out there and the phantom with the number seven on his back gets the ball. Unlike most other players he does not try to avoid you, comes wriggling his casual way towards you. You tense yourself and watch the ball. Now he's within your reach and he sways outward to his right, like a snake. He's going down the wing, you think, and lunge forward with your left foot to block the ball. All of a sudden – Whsst! – this blur goes past you on the inside and your eyes pop-up in amazement.

. . . He's got the ball again – but this time you are ready for him. He's not going to get away with that again. So, as he sways leisurely outwards to his right again, you tackle forward, this time with your right foot to stop him coming inside and – Whsst! – the blur goes past you on the outside . . .

Next time round you are more careful, but – Whsst! – he's much too fast and you are chasing the blur again . . .

. . . Then – Whsst! – there he goes again, and you are lying on the ground and saying to yourself: 'To hell with it. I've had enough of this fellow.'

Danny Blanchflower's Soccer Book

Activities

– Read the sports pages of a newspaper. When you have decided which reports are good, try to write down a list of rules for a successful sports report.
– After watching a sporting contest – not necessarily football – write a newspaper report, obeying the rules you worked out in the previous activity.
– 'The Goal.' Write a short story with this title.
– Football matches have attracted bad publicity, not for the matches but for the hooliganism amongst spectators. If you were Minister for Sport what steps would you take to remedy the situation? You could send a letter to your local paper with your suggestions.
– Read *Goalkeepers are Different* by Brian Glanville.

Nuts and Bolts

There are three writers quoted here; Stubbes, Yevtushenko and Blanchflower. They have different **aims** in putting pen to paper; what are these aims? It is possible for a writer to have more than one.

What would a modern writer use instead of: fellowly, fashion, very hardly, no marvel, choler, effusion? You can guess most of them.

In the word 'intrigue', the **u** shows that the **g** is hard, as in 'begun'. Think of another word with this -**gue** ending.

Unit 21

Personal letters

Villa Igea,
Villa di Gargnano,
Lago di Garda, Italy.
Friday, 6th October, 1912

Dear Mac,

Your books came today, your letter long ago. Now I am afraid I put you to a lot of trouble and expense, and feel quite guilty. But thanks a thousand times. . .

Today it is so stormy. The lake is dark, and with white lambs all over it. The steamer rocks as she goes by. There are no sails stealing past. The vines are yellow and red, and fig trees are in flame on the mountains . . . Yesterday F. and I went down along the lake towards Maderno. We climbed down from a little olive wood, and swam. It was evening, so weird, and a great black cloud trailing over the lake. And tiny little lights of villages came out, so low down, right across the water. Then great lightnings split out. . .

I go in a little place to drink wine near Bogliaco. It is the living-room of the house. The father, sturdy as these Italians are, gets up from table and bows to me. The family is having supper. He brings me red wine to another table, then sits down again, and the mother ladles his soup from the bowl. He has his shirt-sleeves rolled up and his shirt collar open. Then he nods and 'click-clicks' to the small baby, that the mother, young and proud, is feeding with soup from a big spoon. The grandfather, white-moustached, sits a bit effaced by the father. A little girl eats soup. The grandmother by the big, open fire sits and quietly scolds another little girl. It reminds me so of home when I was a boy. They are all so warm with life. The father reaches his thick brown hand to play with the baby – the mother looks quickly away, catching my eye. Then he gets up to wait on me. . .

Why can't you ever come? You could if you wanted to, at Christmas. Why not? We should love to have you, and it costs little. . .

So wrote D.H. Lawrence to his friend, A.W. McLeod. For reasons of space we have not printed the whole letter. Lawrence's letter begins, as many personal letters do, with straightforward details, very often just acknowledging that something has arrived safely. But this letter goes beyond that; clear description helps us sense what the landscape and weather are like, and then the account of the Italian family at supper helps us share the scene with him. Lawrence keeps it in the present tense to make it feel more immediate. And the letter ends with an invitation to stay.

Since this letter was written, the writing of personal letters has declined. A major factor must be the influence of the telephone; it is so much easier and quicker – though often more expensive. The telephone is particularly important if you wish to make arrangements, as you don't have to wait a day or so for a reply. And to hear someone's voice, of course, can be exciting.

Letter-writing is a valuable skill. When family or friends are separated from each other, a good letter can make all the difference. So, what makes a good letter? As you will see from Lawrence's letter to his friend, it is the ability to convey an idea of people, incidents, and description; Lawrence is observant and invites us to be so, too. In writing to friends give plenty of news of what you have been seeing and doing, the places you have visited, the people you have met, and any amusing incidents that have occurred. You should also show an interest in the affairs of the person to whom you are writing.

A personal letter is like a one-sided conversation, in tone. Nevertheless, though it will probably have the ring of speech about it, to write properly, you will need to give the letter some shape and to think carefully about the content.

Some personal letters are more formal than those sent to friends and family. Imagine yourself in this position. Your father is working away from home; your mother is in bed with flu; your young brother is also ill and has been away from school for the last two days. Your mother asks you to write a letter to his school explaining the absence. It might go like this:

10 Orchard Road
Appleton,
AP3 9QA
19th November 1986

Dear Mrs Potter,

I am writing for my mother, who is ill, to explain Stephen's absence.

He has been ill in bed with a high temperature and sore throat. We hope he will be well enough to return to school at the beginning of next week.

Yours sincerely,

Jill Bramley

Note these points:

The *address* is given in full. By tradition in a personal letter, it slants.

The *date* is given underneath the address.

The *start* is 'Dear Mr/Mrs/Miss/Ms. . .' and the *ending* 'Yours sincerely,' (capital *Y*, small *s*, comma). To friends or family you start with 'Dear Jim/Uncle . . .' and you will probably want to finish with one of these:

With best wishes,
With kind regards,
Love from,
Yours,

(Note the comma following each one.)
The *signature* should be level and legible.
The *address* on the envelope will look like this:

Mrs B. Potter,
Ribstone Primary School,
Pippin Road,
APPLETON,
AP4 2RS

Note that about two inches are left at the top for the stamp and cancellation. It is a common mistake to put the address too high up; you risk it being partly blotted out by the cancellation. Sorting and delivery are made easier if you use capitals for the town and by remembering to use the post code.

Activities

– The best activity is to write real letters, so write to a cousin or some other relative or friend you have not seen for some time. Is there someone you know who is ill and who would welcome a letter? For

'. . . none will hear the postman's knock
Without a quickening of the heart.
For who can bear to feel himself forgotten?'

You may remember this from 'Night Mail' in Volume 1.
– Do you have a pen-friend? Some schools have pen-friend schemes for writing to those of your age in schools abroad, not necessarily in a foreign language. It is a useful way of finding out about other people and their customs.
– Dip into D.H. Lawrence's *Selected Letters*. They contain some excellent passages – how he scrubbed the floor, an Italian version of *Hamlet*, being in bed with a bad cold, and so on. In a year or two's time you may enjoy the *Selected Letters* of John Keats.

Nuts and Bolts

Notice the way in which Lawrence sets the scene; we can see the light, the colour and the movement. Find an example for each element. And notice the **tone**, the attitude of the writer to the reader, at the beginning and the end; it is friendly without being gushing.

The words 'the fig trees are in flame' contain a **metaphor**. Turn it into a simile; you'll need to say **like** or **as if**.

Find the **semi-colon** in the paragraph beginning 'Letter-writing is a valuable skill.' Why do you think it is placed here, rather than a comma or full-stop?

Note the use of **strokes** (/) and **dots** in the instructions – to indicate alternatives, and to show that the letter is being continued.

Remember the spelling of: separate, carefully, particularly, occurred.

Unit 22

Business letters

At some stage we all have to write formal letters that come under the general heading of *business* letters. These are the letters we write to suggest to the local council how improvements may be made to a sports ground, to apply for a job, to request information, to complain, and so on.

Imagine this is an advertisement you have come across in the newspaper:

A letter might go like this:

19 Brantwood Avenue,
WHEELHAM
BH3 6CG
17th November 1986

Ben's Best BMX Bikes,
14 High Street,
HOPTON,
HP7 3PQ

Dear Sir,

I have seen your advertisement in the *Daily Standard* and would like a copy of the free brochure, please.

Yours faithfully,

David Taylor

The secret in writing business letters is quite simple: be clear, be brief, be polite. A rude or muddled request will be put on one side. And when it comes to applying for a job, the applicant's letter is at first the only thing an employer knows about him or her. It is too early to discuss letters of application for jobs, but when the time comes, don't hesitate to ask your English teacher for guidance.

Imagine you have an elder sister who sent by post for a home perm kit that has not arrived. She says you are better at writing letters than she is and you agree to write one for her, thus:

19 Brantwood Avenue,
WHEELHAM,
BH3 6CG
17th November 1986

The Everperm Co. (S10c),
Wave Way Trading Estate,
WESTPOOL,
WP10 3TN

Dear Sirs,

Three weeks ago I sent you £3.80 for your No. 1 Everperm Kit, which was a special offer in *Girl*, 25th October, but it has not arrived.

May I please have it as soon as possible?

Yours faithfully,

Karen Taylor

A possible reply might be:

The Everperm Co.
Wave Way Trading Estate
WESTPOOL
WP10 3TN
Ref PN/EM
19 November 1986

Miss Karen Taylor
19 Brantwood Avenue
WHEELHAM
BH3 6CG

Dear Miss Taylor

No. 1 Everperm Kit

Thank you for your letter of 17 November 1986 concerning the special offer on our No. 1 Everperm Kit.

There was such a good response to our offer that we are temporarily out of stock, but we hope to obtain and despatch the kit to you within the next 28 days. We apologise for any inconvenience caused.

We hope you will accept the enclosed voucher for 50p off the price of our Evercurl Heated Styling Brush, details of which are printed on the voucher.

Yours sincerely

P. Newton, Sales Manager

There are many different styles of business letter with each firm having its own individual system of punctuation and layout. Some will have commas in addresses, others won't; some will have the paragraphs indented, others won't indent but will have a double space between paragraphs; some will put your name and address at the top, some at the bottom. There is no hard and fast rule, except that the letter must be clear, neat, and well presented, with a space either side, top and bottom, to prevent the letter looking cramped.

Note these points:
The *address* is in full, as for personal letters.
The *date* is given underneath the address.
The *start* is 'Dear Sir or Madam' or 'Dear Sirs', the usual form of addressing a company.
The *content* gives the information clearly and briefly. Remember that people are busy. And don't forget: one paragraph for each topic.
The *ending* is 'Yours faithfully,' (capital *Y*, small *f*) for a letter beginning 'Dear Sir(s) or Madam'.
The name of the *company addressed* is given in full.

Activities

– As we said in the previous unit, the best activity is to write real letters. Look through a paper or magazine and find an advertisement about which you would like some more information or which asks readers to write for details.
– If you nearly fell off your bike because of a pot-hole near the kerb, or you think there are ways of improving the amenities for young people in your area, write a letter to the local council.
– Collect all the replies to business letters you send – and ask to see any other business letters that arrive at your home – to see the various styles of layout.

Nuts and Bolts

Look at the first two **paragraphs** of the unit, and the paragraph beginning 'There are many different styles. . .'. Do the opening sentences of each paragraph make good introductions to the rest of the paragraph?

A reminder that **punctuation** and **order** matter. Do not make the mistake of the builder who sent in a bill 'To taking up floor to find dead rat and replacing same, £10.50.'

In this unit there are three words for doers: employer, teacher, manager. Adding **-er** is the normal way of making a doer word. But a number of such words have had their doer ending attached before they came into use here, because they are of French or Latin origin: doctor, radiator, inspector, surveyor, tractor. Have a guess at the doer words from: plant, eject, deposit, dig; and check your results with your dictionary.

Say these words carefully, syllable by syllable: business, temporarily, inconvenience, individual, punctuation.

Unit 23

The robots' revolt

A small American town, well equipped with robots, is dominated by the Pastor, who runs a chapel complete with his own prayer-book and scriptures. But he is harsh and repressive to his children, Hez and Abi, and makes an invalid of his wife. The latest model robot, Max, realizes that the human beings are making a mess of things, and calls a meeting of the robots, at which they communicate by plugging in to each other. Eventually all ends well, with the Pastor's wife restored to health and vigour, while the Pastor himself leaves the town, never to return:

The robots came.

The Mk Is wheeled along in their ungainly, lumpish way, clumsy mobile boxes. The Mk IIs strode rheumatically, overtaking the Mk Is, gleaming, reflecting the sun, swinging their legs and hips.

Max was the only robot absent from the march. Nobody noticed this, however, for nobody knew that a rally was about to take place. The robots had, as usual, asked permission to leave their homes for a short time and the permission had, as usual, been given. Robots often took time off to attend to their own (or more likely the family's) affairs outside the house. A robot could work a 24-hour day. Some did. Their human masters and mistresses felt it only reasonable that such hard-working servants should have time off when it was requested.

The robots gathered under the largest tree of Gospel Square. There were about two hundred of them: one for every human of the community. They stood shoulder to shoulder in neat ranks fanning out from the big old tree. Some rested their fingers on others' shoulders to 'talk'; the talk was silent, a direct communication – a plug-in. Most just stood, silent and motionless.

Humans gathered round, curious. . .

The lone figure of Max, glittering coppery gold, strode through the humans. They made way for him: their eyes followed him. But no robot head turned and no robot body moved.

Max deliberately made his way to the great tree, the focal point of the square. Easily, gracefully, he raised himself so that he stood on the slatted seat ringing the tree trunk. Now he stood higher than the assembled robots facing him. In the shade, the inner light of his eyes seemed to glare. He stood without moving. Human voices buzzed: and became silent.

Max raised his right hand and touched his neck with it.

At last there were sounds from the robots, a harsh whisper like a wind through metallic grass as robot arms were raised and robot fingers found the necks of their neighbours and rested there.

Now the robots were one. . .

Then he shouted.

The shout was a single bellowing note like a trumpet blast. The reply was the same sound multiplied by hundreds: a short, blaring, defiant, triumphant, brazen yell that shook windows, stirred the leaves on the great tree and rocked the humans.

Max was speaking – but soundlessly. You knew he was addressing the robots only because his hands and head moved to emphasize his words – and because the words stirred his audience, linked hand to neck. Sometimes you could see a slight surge forward of robot bodies; sometimes, the stillness of complete attention; then another little movement, another surge, detectable only because the slanting sun magnified the small movements of the robots' heads.

The man standing by Hez swore softly to himself, then said, 'If only we could hear just what that devil's saying.'

As he spoke, so did Max. 'Hear me!' cried his brazen voice – a huge voice that Abi and Hez never knew existed. 'Listen to me, you humans! I speak for all my race: not only for myself but for all robots. I speak of peace and understanding and salvation – IF.'

'IF!' shouted the robots – not as humans would have replied, in a straggling volley, but with one sound, like the shot from a gun.

'I speak in your own tongue,' Max continued, 'so that all may understand. I can tell you that there is to be a new beginning and a new end to your history, human history. The beginning is now. The end is soon. None of you will suffer, all of you will gain – IF.'

'IF!' shouted the robots. The humans gaped and were silent.

'IF you listen to the voice of Reason! If and only if! Consider: since man first stood upright and learned to make fire and speak words, his race has ruled this Earth,' said Max, speaking less loudly now. 'Man conquered the land and sea and the skies above him – even space. You have conquered nearly every living thing inhabiting Earth.

'But – *but* – you have not conquered yourselves! And unless –'

'UNLESS!' shouted the robots.

'Unless you listen to the voice of Reason – the voice you yourselves created – the voice you are hearing now –'

'LISTEN!' the robots shouted.

But people no longer listened. Heads turned to a ripple of disturbance as the crowd parted to let through the black-hatted, square-shouldered, grim figure of the Pastor.

Robot Revolt:
Nicholas Fisk

Comment

The robots in the passage have powers far beyond those ever likely to be found in actual machines. In fact they have some of the abilities of a human brain – which is an organism of incredible complexity and efficiency. But the fact that the tale is about impossibilities does not spoil it in the least; the story is a good one, and has a point to it. Nicholas Fisk puts into Max's 'mouth' something that he himself wants to say to his readers. The world, Max declares, needs 'peace and understanding and salvation'; and to gain these it must start afresh. Because, in spite of conquering every living thing, men have not conquered themselves.

Activities

– What is there in the activities of men that needs to be conquered, do you think? Jot down your thoughts.
– You will have thought about robots already in Unit 2 of Volume 2, and you may have followed our recommendation and read *Robot Revolt*. What dangers do you see occurring from the increasing use of robots? And what good things? Set your answers out as two lists.
– Write a short newspaper article, of 150 words, about the meeting of robots.
– Write a story in which a robot (who cannot speak) attempts to teach a fifteen-year-old not to be untidy.
– Try some of the science fiction of H.G. Wells: *The War of the Worlds* or *The Time Machine*.

Nuts and Bolts

At the very end of the piece the author might have written 'Heads turned to a **movement** of disturbance' instead of '. . . a **ripple** of disturbance . . .'. What did the writer gain by saying 'ripple'?

Note the spelling of: stillness, detectable, and magnified.

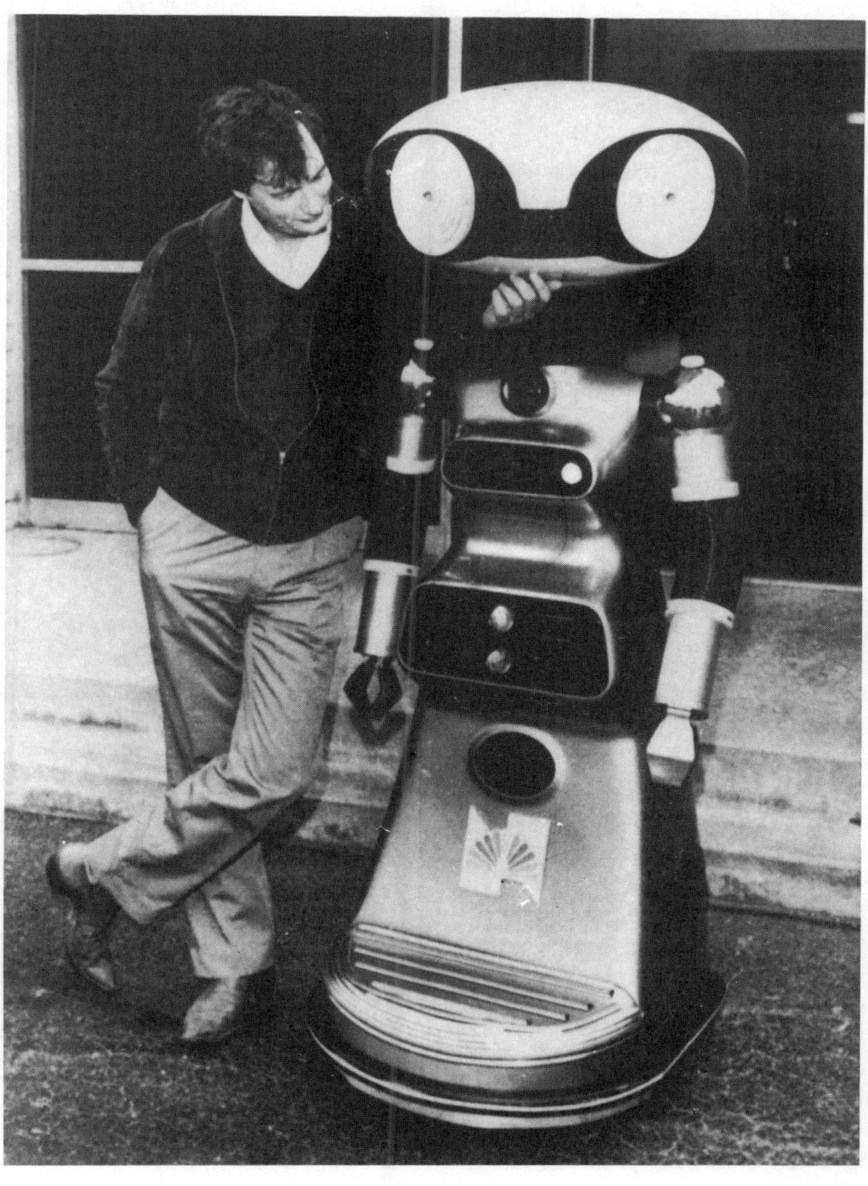

Unit 24

It pays to advertise

Read these four advertisements, made up for printing here:

1 Are you going grey too early?
There's no need to let grey hair make you look older than you are. The well-known Carey Course, based on a fabulous scientific formula, is the safe and easy answer to the problem that has worried millions of men and women.

2 It's smart to drink gin
Gin is a guest at the smartest and most sophisticated parties. Serve gin in all or any of a dozen welcome ways and make sure your party's a success. Get with the best people and buy a bottle today!

3 Millions of discriminating families insist on Zephyr. No ordinary soap brings such a thrilling all-over freshness to your skin! There's all the sparkle of spring in country-fresh Zephyr. It keeps you cool and fragrant all day long – as fresh and invigorating as the dawn breeze of a summer's day.

4 Get ahead with a Lynx!
Distinctive styling and superb performance make the Lynx the leader in modern motoring. Those in the know realize that its achievement has that indefinable quality recognized by generations of discerning drivers.

Now take them one at a time; and imagine that you are a person who responds and buys what is offered. What is it about each ad that gets hold of the reader and persuades him or her to act?

Next time you watch commercial television, note down what is on offer in one of the advertising slots. Notice also what kinds of goods are proclaimed on big posters. Pick up a newspaper, look at the large, 'displayed' advertisements, and again note down what sorts of things they want us to buy.

Most of the many millions spent on advertising goes on the television spots, posters and displayed columns in the press. They are successful – people would not pay for them if they weren't. And the secret of their success is that they get us to stop thinking and give way to our feelings and emotions. Just as we are thinking of putting 50p aside towards that new cassette or fishing rod, we are tricked into spending it: 'Give yourself a treat and buy a couple of Bettabars – now!' Your parents may be got at in a similar fashion by appeals to self-indulgence: 'After a busy day at work, you well deserve a . . .'.

A lot of advertising tries to persuade people to buy one of two almost identical items, such as two brands of beer, two small cars, two kinds of soap. In such comparisons there is not much to be argued about; there really is not much to be said in favour of one cigarette as opposed to another. So advertising does not use much in the way of plain argument. Moreover arguments and well-chosen evidence are dull; no one wants to read such stuff. Advertisements must never, never be dull. That would be fatal.

What then do we get instead of evidence, facts and argument? Various things, one of which is glamour:

Glamour for the modern girl
Created for you by a leading Paris
designer to bring out your personality

This dreamy two-piece suit can be
yours for only £ . . . from Susan
Superstyles

Glamour is often turned on in car advertising and travel blurbs such as:

Your stay in this most exotic
land of the magical East will leave
you rich in golden memories

The idea is to link a product with thrills, romance, getting right away from the humdrum daily round.

'Glamour is often turned on in car advertising . . .'

For this reason smoking is shown against a background of lovely streams and beautiful forests; drinking goes on in the warmth and cosy comfort of happy social occasions at home or in a pub; and numerous products are seen in the hands of well-dressed people at their ease in a luxury background. In addition, some of these adverts work on our feelings of snobbishness, when they invite us to join an exclusive social set.

A similar method is for advertisements to flatter their readers, like this one (for a food) aimed at parents:

> Talented children need extra care

and again in phrases such as: 'Particular people prefer . . .', 'The choice of the privileged few . . .' and 'Those in the know go for . . .'. Yet others work on the feeling which we all have of wanting to be like other human beings, and to be in their company. So we hear: 'Millions of satisfied users . . .', 'The great majority choose . . .' and 'Found in every home . . .'. However a thing is not necessarily good just because a lot of people have bought it. That fear of being different is not the only fear that is stirred up by advertising. It is the fear of getting old, tired, ill, ugly or depressed that sells night drinks, nerve tonics, smell banishers, hair restorers and so on.

The advertisements we've been considering succeed, because they are big, clever, bright-coloured, noisy, won't take no for an answer and get right inside us. However there is a form of advertising which uses none of these methods. That is, the classified advertising we see in the evening papers, weeklies and specialist magazines like *Exchange and Mart*. They give us information about things for sale, things wanted or lost, sometimes houses, jobs and services like plumbing and television repairs. The individual ads take up little space and there is no big print and no pictures. Do you see why they are called 'classified?'

What we have to remember is that there is no connection between the quality of a product and the way it is advertised. Clever and amusing ads tell us nothing about the thing on sale; at the same time we may very much dislike the advertisements for something which is really good.

Comment

Advertising is a big part of modern life, and it costs us a lot of money, but that is not the reason why we have included it. The point is that, though advertising uses pictures a good deal, it cannot get far without *words* – for the name of the product, for slogans about it, and for persuading the possible purchaser. Our concern is with words; the way they are used; and the aims of writers in using them.

Activities

– Cut out six full-page colour advertisements from a magazine. The Sunday newspaper colour supplements are ideal for this – though make sure you are not going to offend anyone in the family who has not yet read the magazine. For each advertisement, note
(i) any factual information (price, size, etc)
(ii) what fears and feelings are being exploited.
– Design and write an advertisement for this book!
– Take a copy of a newspaper and, by calculating the area of each advertisement, work out the proportion of space the paper allots to advertisements.
– Look at one particular television advertisement and note, very quickly, the various scenes, the type of person or people, and what the advert suggests the product will do for you. This is very much easier if you have a video-cassette recorder.
– Take an honest look at the part advertising plays in your life, particularly in the world of fashion.

Nuts and Bolts

What was the **aim** of the writer in the passage above? The last three paragraphs will help you to answer. An answer of two or three lines will be quite enough.

You will probably write out a small advertisement for the classified columns of a paper one day. When you do, be careful about **order** and **punctuation**, and make sure your ad cannnot be taken the wrong way, like this one:

> Double-action harp for sale, suitable for a lady in perfect condition.

Unit 25

Lila

Early morning in an Indian village:

When Lila went out on the beach it was so early in the morning that there was no one else there. The sand was washed clean by last night's tide and no one had walked on it except the birds that fished along the coast. She walked down to the sea with the small basket, filled with flowers she had plucked from the garden around their house.

When she came to the edge of the sea, she lifted the folds of her sari and waded out into the waves that came rushing up over her feet and swirling about her ankles in creamy foam. She waded in till she came to the sacred rock, a kind of temple in the sea. Lila took the flowers from her basket and scattered them about the rock, then folded her hands and bowed.

Later in the morning more women would come and offer flowers at the sacred rock. Some would say a little prayer for the safety of the fisherman at sea because they were all the wives and daughters of fisherman. It seemed a good way to start the morning.

When Lila's father still owned a boat and went to sea to fish, her mother used to bring flowers to this rock in the sea, and pray. But he no longer fished, he had sold his boat to pay his debts, her mother was too ill and weak to get out of her bed, and it was Lila who came to begin the morning with an offering of flowers to the sea. Sometimes she felt it was the best time of day for her, the only perfectly happy and peaceful one. Emptying out the last petals from her basket, she turned and walked back up the beach to the line of coconut palms now gilded by the sun. It was time to start work.

But when Lila came to the log that bridged the swampy creek and led to their hut on the other bank, she looked at the hut and knew that nothing was as it had been before, and nothing was well either. The hut should have been re-thatched years ago – the old palm leaves were dry and tattered and slipping off the beams. The earthen walls were crumbling. The windows gaped, without any shutters. There was no smoke to be seen curling up from under a cooking pot on a fire, as in the other huts.

Her two sisters stood at the door brushing their teeth with twigs they had broken off the tree at the back. They had not washed or changed for school. When she called to them, 'Why don't you dress? You'll be late for school,' they answered, 'But you haven't even made us our tea yet – *you're* late.'

Lila threw down the little basket at the door and

went in to make a fire. She knew she ought to do it before she went to the beach. Then she could put on the pot of water and have it boiling when she came back. But somehow, when she woke up in the morning, she felt she had to flee to the beach: she couldn't face the dirty cooking pots of the night before until she had been out on the beach. Now she had been there, she would collect firewood, light it and make tea for the family. She wished Bela and Kamal would understand.

She made their tea silently. The three sisters sat on their heels, waiting for it to boil and for their brother to bring them some milk.

They sat on the threshold, looking down the path that led through the coconut grove and soon they saw Hari coming along with a small brass pot of milk. Unlike the two little girls, he had washed and was dressed in clean khaki shorts and a shirt. The small girls ran to take the milk from him. Lila poured some into the pot, and soon it was ready.

'What about father and mother?' asked Hari.

'I'll take mother's glass to her,' said Lila.

'But father's asleep,' said Bela and Kamal together.

Hari's head sank low as he stared at the empty tumbler while Lila pushed and shoved and made her sisters change into their blue skirts and white blouses that all the school-girls in the village wore, and found their few tattered books with which they set off for school.

Lila went in with a tumbler of tea for her mother. She stopped to add a little extra milk to it. Then she went past the curtain in the doorway to the room where her mother lay on the string bed on some old grey sheets. She herself looked like a crumpled grey rag lying there. She had been ill for a long time. No one knew what was wrong. She had no pains and no fever but simply grew weaker and weaker all the time. Now she could not sit up to drink her tea. Lila had to lift her head and help her drink in little sips from the tumbler. She was very gentle and careful because her mother seemed so frail one hardly liked to touch her.

She also kept her head turned away from the heap that lay on a mat in a corner of the dark, shadowy room. The heap did not stir but made a grumbling sound of obstructed breathing and also stank. Lila could smell the fermented toddy even from a distance – it was a smell she had known and hated since she was a small girl. She kept her nose wrinkled up and wished her father would throw himself into some other corner to sleep and not foul her mother's room with the stench of drunkenness. But no one dared tell him, least of all her mother.

All she said was, 'Lila, have the girls gone to school?'

'Yes.'

'And Hari to the fields?'

'Yes, Hari to the fields.'

'Then you must sweep and go to market and cook.'

'Yes, Ma,' said Lila, although she did not need to be told. She had given up going to school long ago, so that she could stay home and do the cooking and washing and look after the others. She got up to start.

The Village by the Sea:
Anita Desai

Comment

Lila is a remarkable girl, full of common sense, who has to act responsibly and make important decisions for her family. It is no easy task keeping them fed and looked after.

The story from which this is taken is based on life in a village – a real village – on the western coast of India.

The book won the *Guardian* Fiction Award.

Activities

– Lila's early morning visit to the beach 'seemed a good way to start the morning'. Make a note of why you think this is so.
– Make a list of the hardships that confront Lila each day.
– Imagine that Lila had joined a pen-friend scheme and that her letter to you had contained some of the information in this extract. Write her a letter in reply, thinking very carefully not only of what you want to tell her about yourself, but also of the *tone* you would adopt; you would have to avoid being patronizing. (Look up the meaning of 'patronizing' if you are unsure of its precise sense.)
– If Lila came to spend four or five days with your family, what events would you organize?
– Read the novel; you will find it moving.

Nuts and Bolts

Find the paragraph 'Lila went in . . .' and write it but with the sentences on separate lines and mixing up the order.

Look back at Unit 11, and put the jumbled paragraph in the right order. Check your results.

In the fourth paragraph we read 'gilded by the sun'. The first or literal meaning of 'gilded' is 'covered with gold leaf', but that is not its meaning here. What is?

Link **there** (meaning in that place) with **here** and **where**.

Note: peace**ful**, care**ful**, drunke**nness**, unti**l**.

Unit 26

Hari fends for himself

Lila's brother, Hari, knew that he had to break out of a life of poverty. He decides to try his luck in Bombay:

He was silenced by awe when he saw the city of Bombay looming over their boats and the oily green waves. He would have liked to stand and stare as he disembarked from the boat, aching and stiff from the long ride in the jam-packed boat, but there was no time, no leisure for that. His fellow passengers were pushing and shoving and jostling past him and he was carried along by them. They pushed and shoved because they were in turn being pushed and shoved by the Bombay crowds that thronged the docks – people in a hurry to get something done, so many people in such a great hurry as the villagers had never seen before. It was only out of the corner of his eye that he saw, briefly, before being pushed on, the great looming sides of steamships berthed at the docks, cranes lifting and lowering huge bales, men bare-bodied and sweating carrying huge packing cases, boxes and baskets on their heads and shoulders, grunting as they hurried, women like the fisherwomen at home with their purple and green saris tucked up as they ran with baskets of shining, slithering fish from the boats to the market, straw and mud and fish scales making the ground dangerously slippery. Added to this chaos were the smells of the city mingling with the familiar smells of the sea and fish and turning them into something strange, and the noises of the city – not only the familiar fishermen's voices, loud and ringing, but the noise of the traffic which was so rarely heard in or around Thul.

And now they were out through the gates and on the street and in the midst of the terrifying traffic. In all his life Hari had not seen so much traffic as he saw in that one moment on that one street. In Thul there was only an occasional bus driving down the main road of the village to the highway, and very rarely a single, dusty car. When he went to Alibagh, it was

Bombay docks

chiefly bicycles that he saw, and a few cycle-rickshaws, and of course buses and lorries. But here there was everything at once as if all the traffic in the world had met on the streets of Bombay – cycles, rickshaws, hand-carts, tongas, buses, cars, taxis and lorries – hooting and screeching and grinding and roaring past and around him.

[After some time, and feeling very hungry, Hari is taken to a cheap restaurant.]

The Sri Krishna Eating House was the meanest and shabbiest restaurant Hari had ever seen: even in Thul and along the highway there were cafes that were pleasanter; usually wooden shacks built in the shade of a mango or frangipani tree with a handful of marigolds and hibiscus crammed into an old ink bottle for a vase, coloured cigarette packets and bottles of aerated drinks attractively arranged on the shelves, and possibly a bright picture of a god or goddess on the wall with a tinsel garland around the frame and heavily scented joss sticks burning before it.

When Hari said next morning – after being handed a tumbler of tea and a rolled up *chapati* without his asking for anything – 'I have no money to pay for all this food you are giving me. Will you let me work in your kitchen instead?' the man considered for only a moment, frowning as he thought. Then he said, 'Yes, I can do with another boy in the kitchen. Start by washing these pots. Then you can knead the dough and help roll out the *chapatis*. If you like, you can stay here and work for your meals and – uh – one rupee a day, like the other boys.'

So Hari went to work in the small kitchen at the back of the eating house. He saw there was nothing to scour the pots with except some blackened coconut husks and the ash from the fires, and he did the best he could with them although Lila would certainly not have considered the results good enough. Later he helped the two boys knead great hills of dough in their pans and this was hard work and made them grunt and sweat.

The Village by the Sea:
Anita Desai

Comment

Hari's struggle to cope with a harsh life is rewarded: it teaches him to be resourceful; and he is befriended by a neighbouring shopkeeper, a watch-repairer, who teaches Hari how to clean and mend watches, thus giving him a skill that will serve him well later.

Activities

– Describe a busy scene that you have witnessed, with people shoving and jostling. It need not be a scene by docks, as here; it could be a jumble sale or the queue for a football match.
– Write a poem suggested by the description of the Sri Krishna Eating House.
– Imagine the dialogue between Hari and Lila, on his eventual return to the village, about his work in the kitchen of the café. What would Hari have told her?
– How do you view Hari's decision to 'fend for himself'? Was it courageous to leave his village and the life of poverty? Or was it cruel to leave Lila to look after the family? Perhaps it was a mixture of both? Should he have told Lila he was going? Jot down your response.
– The most important aspect of growing up is to leave home and be independent; we must all learn to fend for ourselves. What thoughts do you have about this?

Nuts and Bolts

In the description of the docks in the second half of the first paragraph, four of the **senses** are brought in to present a vivid picture. What are they?

Find the paragraph 'It was certainly. . .' and look at the way **dashes** are used. Then – with one of these words: contradict, expand, discuss, refute, explain – fill in the gap in this sentence: 'The words preceded by a dash, or bracketed by dashes, ------ what the writer has just said'.

Make **adjectives** from: fun, dog, grit, cat. And from: bone, fate, anger, speed.

Unit 27

In a hole full of snakes

MacTootle told Gerald Durrell of a drainage pit full of snakes worth adding to his collection. It was dark when they reached the pit, crawling with young Gaboon vipers, 'one of the most deadly snakes in the world'. They are sluggish by day but very lively at night. Durrell was afraid of being lowered into the twelve feet deep hole, but did not like to back out. 'I have rarely regretted a decision more.':

Drearily I approached the pit. My audience was clustered round, twittering in delicious anticipation. I tied the rope round my waist with what I very soon discovered was a slip-knot, and crawled to the edge. My descent had not the airy grace of a pantomine fairy; the sides of the pit were so crumbly that every time I tried to gain a foothold I dislodged large quantities of earth, and as this fell among the snakes it was greeted with peevish hisses. I had to dangle in mid-air, being gently lowered by my companions, while the slip-knot grasped me ever tighter round the waist. Eventually I looked down and I saw that my feet were a yard from the ground. I shouted to my friends to stop lowering me, as I wanted to examine the ground I was to land on and make sure there were no snakes lying there. After a careful inspection I could not see any reptiles directly under me, so I shouted 'Lower away' in what I sincerely hoped was an intrepid tone of voice. As I started on my descent again, two things happened at once: first, one of my borrowed shoes fell off and, secondly, the lamp, which none of us had remembered to pump up, died away to a faint glow of light, rather like a plump cigar-end. At that precise moment I touched ground with my bare foot, and I cannot remember ever having been so frightened, before or since.

I stood motionless, sweating with great freedom, while the lamp was hastily hauled up to the surface, pumped up, and lowered down again. I have never been so glad to see a humble pressure-lamp. Now the pit was once more flooded with lamp-light I began to feel a little braver. I retrieved my shoe and put it on, and this made me feel even better. I grasped my stick in a moist hand and approached the nearest snake. I pinned it to the ground with the forked end, picked it up and put it in the bag. This part of the procedure gave me no qualms, for it was simple enough and not dangerous provided you exercised a certain care. The idea is to pin the reptile across the head with the fork and then get a good firm grasp on its neck before picking it up. What worried me was the fact that while my attention was occupied with one snake, all the others were wriggling round frantically, and I had to keep a cautious eye open in case one got behind me and I stepped back on it. They were beautifully marked with an intricate pattern of brown, silver, pink and cream blotches, and when they remained still this coloration made them extremely hard to see; they just melted into the background. As soon as I pinned one to the ground, it would start to hiss like a kettle, and all the others would hiss in sympathy – a most unpleasant sound.

There was one nasty moment when I bent down to pick up one of the reptiles and heard a loud hissing apparently coming from somewhere horribly close to my ear. I straightened up and found myself staring into a pair of angry silver-coloured eyes approximately a foot away. After considerable juggling I managed to get this snake down on the ground and pin him beneath my stick. On the whole, the reptiles were just as scared of me as I was of them, and they did their best to get out of my way. It was only when I had them cornered that they fought and struck viciously at the stick, but bounced off the brass fork with a reassuring ping. However, one of them must have been more experienced, for he ignored the brass fork and bit instead at the wood. He got a good grip and hung on like a bull-dog; he would not let go even when I lifted him clear of the ground. Eventually I had to shake the stick really hard, and the snake sailed through the air, hit the side of the pit and fell to the ground hissing furiously.

I was down in the pit for about half an hour, and I caught twelve Gaboon vipers; I was not sure, even then, that I had captured all of them, but I felt it would be tempting fate to stay down there any longer. My companions hauled me out, hot, dirty, and streaming with sweat, clutching in one hand a bag of loudly hissing snakes.

'There, now,' said my friend triumphantly, while I was recovering my breath, 'I told you I'd get you some specimens, did I not?'

I just nodded; by that time I was beyond speech. I sat on the ground, smoking a much-needed cigarette and trying to steady my trembling hands. Now that the danger was over I began to realise for the first time how extremely stupid I had been to go into the pit in the first place, and how exceptionally lucky I was to have come out of it alive. I made a mental note that in future, if anyone asked me if animal-collecting was a dangerous occupation, that I would reply that it was only as dangerous as your own stupidity allowed it to be. When I had recovered slightly, I looked about me and discovered that one of my audience was missing.

'Where's your brother got to?' I asked my friend.

'Oh him,' said MacTootle with fine scorn, 'he couldn't watch any more – he said it made him feel sick. He's waiting over there for us. You'll have to excuse him – he couldn't take it. Sure, and it required some guts to watch you down there with all them wretched reptiles.'

Encounters with Animals: Gerald Durrell

Comment

Gerald Durrell is nearly always light-hearted in his writing; he sees the funny side of things. Here though his experience has no funny side; he does not disguise his extreme fright throughout the episode. All the same he gets some fun out of the circumstances. There is just enough said about MacTootle to show what a ridiculously one-sided view of things he had – taking the credit for the capture of the snakes and being quite blind to the danger he had got Durrell into.

Activities

– Have you ever started on something for a dare, after much hesitation, and then felt frightened? If so, tell the story of what happened; and if not, make up a story.
– One day on heath-land a girl runs up to you and says her little sister has been bitten by a snake. What exactly would you do?
– Read any of Gerald Durrell's books. You may recall the two extracts from *My Family and Other Animals* in Volume 2. You could also try Margaret Lane's *Life with Ionides* and William Saroyan's *The Snake*.
– Write a set of questions you would like to ask Gerald Durrell if you were given the opportunity of interviewing him.
– Why is there a snake on the badge of the Royal Army Medical Corps?

Nuts and Bolts

It is useful to get some idea of the meaning of the common prefixes. **Con**, for example, means 'with' or 'together'. In 'dislodged' **dis** can mean 'apart' or 'not'. **In** means 'in', as in 'inspector' (one who looks **in**to things), or 'not', as in 'ineffective'. See if you can find prefixes meaning 'down', 'again', and 'before' (all in the paragraph beginning 'Drearily I approached . . .').

Unit 28

Empty world

Neil believes he is the sole survivor in England of a devastating plague from the East. In the search for other survivors he manages to drive to London, settles in a big West End house, and wanders through Harrods. He finds a footmark in a freshly spilled liquid. He is sure he will find the owner of the print within walking distance of the store:

He started the search next morning, and spent the day driving around. All he achieved was a fuller awareness of what a warren London was; and the unhappy realisation that in guessing her mode of transport he had overlooked a possibility. It could have been a bicycle . . .

It was with this in mind that he had what he thought was a brainwave. He remembered the dinging bells of burglar alarms, harshly calling attention to themselves. They had depended on electric power, but there was something that didn't, and would be heard over a far greater area.

The first church he found was equipped with an electrical bell system, but the second had ropes. He heaved on one and heard the bell clang out high above. He rang and rang, pulling until his arms were sore; then found a pew and sat down. Sparrows had found a way in before him and chattered up in the rafters . . .

Neil thought of the acres of interlocking streets, the vast area within easy cycling distance of the store. There must be a way of limiting the range. The thing to remember was that she had been facing the same problems as himself, and had very likely come to similar solutions. He had chosen Princes Gate for comfort, and for access to a good supply of fresh water. Was there an alternative location, offering the same possibilities?

He did not have to think long: the answer was obvious. The best water supply possible – better than the Serpentine – was the Thames. And riverside Chelsea abounded in comfortable houses. That was where he should concentrate his search.

Neil took rations for several days, and spare batteries for his torch. He picked out his sturdiest pair of shoes, but on reflection abandoned them in favour of some with crepe soles. It was not too cold – grey but mild – but he crammed a jersey in. He wanted to be prepared for a long expedition.

He passed through the museums area of South Kensington on his way, and remembered Saturday afternoons, and ice-creams sold from barrows. The gutters were choked and the forecourt of the tube station, where the paperboys had shouted, was thick with accumulated dirt and rubbish. He trudged on south, to Sloane Square and the King's Road . . .

The big private houses near the river were the best bet, and he headed that way. But there were so many of them, so many once-affluent tree-lined streets. He studied the houses he passed for signs of occupancy. If she were avoiding people she would probably try not to leave any, but something might give her away. He thought he was on to something when he saw a trail worn across what had once been a small lawn, but it led him to a large hole under a wall – a fox's earth most likely. . .

Three more days of fruitless tramping followed. He was discouraged, and wondered if he could have guessed wrong about the district. She might not have had his idea about a fresh water supply, or she might have picked a different stretch of the river bank. The south side, perhaps, even though the houses were smaller and less luxurious there.

His luck changed unexpectedly. He had finished the provisions in his haversack; he thought of going back home, but decided it would be easier to forage near at hand. He went to the nearest supermarket in the King's Road, and smashed a way in. There was plenty of food, but also sections of shelf which had been stripped. He looked more closely and saw the signs of a recent human presence: dust disturbed on the shelves and floor.

Neil followed the track. It led not to the door he had broken, but out to the back. There was a yard, and a steel gate. The gate was padlocked, but the chain had been severed with metal cutters.

From that point all he had to do was to wait. He found an upper room across the street with a view of the gate, drew up a chair to the window, and settled down. He watched carefully all that day, and most of the next.

Even so, he missed her; she had probably entered the store while he was in the bathroom. He looked out to see the gate opening, and at the same time realised he had not noticed an addition to the scene – an old-fashioned lady's bicycle, with a basket in front of the handlebars, leaning against the wall further down.

Neil ran for the stairs. She was getting on the bicycle as he came out of the front door. He did not call, but raced towards her.

She heard him; and without looking round started to pedal away. If she had had another second or two, she would have outdistanced him, but he managed to get close enough to grab the carrier at the back. The metal cut into his fingers and a backward-kicking foot bruised his arm, but he held on. The bicycle swerved, and she fell.

Empty World:
John Christopher

This picture shows the devastation caused by a different sort of bomb.

Comment

This unit comes from the thrilling story of how Neil coped with fear, isolation, danger and death all around him as the plague flashed across the country with terrible speed. He went to London because it seemed to offer the best hope of finding other survivors. He met one who seemed to be mad, and found another who had just killed himself because there seemed no point in going on. The story ends in a way that leaves the reader to fill in a lot for himself.

Activities

– Continue the story. What conversation ensues – and what decisions are made? Try to keep the spirit and tone of the extract.
– Imagine arriving at your home after a day at school and finding no one about. You walk from room to room and then go out into the street. Still no one ...
– A publisher hears that you enjoy reading and sends you this extract to see whether you think publication of the book would be a good idea. Make a note of your feelings and thoughts and say what you think was the author's point in writing it.
– Apart from this extract from *Empty World*, we printed an extract from another book by John Christopher, *The Guardians*, in Volume 1 (Unit 13, 'Rob's new school'). Can you find any similarities between the two extracts?

Nuts and Bolts

Guess or find out the meanings of the **prefixes** in:
interlocking, **con**centrate, **re**flection, **pre**pared, **ex**pedition, **dis**couraged, **un**expectedly.
For example, '**re**vise' means 'look **again**'.

A spelling family that should be known is descended from the Latin word **finis**, meaning 'end' or 'boundary'. Writers used to put it at the end of their books. The family has over twenty members. Here are a few:

finish
final
finite
in**fin**ite
de**fin**ite
con**fine**

Unit 29

Shepherds Bushwhackers

Jodie Bell at fourteen is a star performer in a professional gymnasts team, which has just paid a £250,000 transfer fee for her. In this world of the not-too-distant future, girls are 'sold' at four to gymnastic clubs, starved to the perfect weight and worked to the point of collapse.

Here Beth has had a painful injury but Miss Amey the hard and harsh coach says she is fit to perform for the Bushwhackers. Dr Kennedy is the team doctor, and Derek is a friendly journalist. The Rostova is a complex and difficult movement:

Beth was drawn to go on the beam last. Jodie, one rotation behind her, watched closely as Beth did her floor exercise, a vivacious and spirited performance to the music of *Nut Rocker*. The knee, tightly bandaged, showed no sign of weakness. The crowd went wild – 'Welcome back, welcome back,' they chanted, swaying rhythmically from side to side. Beth Laurence was highly popular among the Whackerbackers; they had missed her.

The gymnasts moved round, and moved round again. The electronic scoreboard computed and flashed the running totals: Bushwhackers 102, Rejects 97.5. A lead of seven clear points was needed if the Bush were to go through to the fourth round. Miss Amey bawled abuse from the sidelines.

Jodie tried to forget that Derek was watching from the Press box. Normally she was glad to see him; today she was unaccountably nervous. She performed two competent vaults, scoring 9.45, and sat down by Maggie. Beth was twirling around the asymmetric bars – she spun off into a piked dismount, landed and sprawled awkwardly on her side. So that was that. Ninety-eight per cent had not been enough. She hobbled off, supported by Miss Amey and Dr Kennedy. Beth was out, and so, probably, was the Bush.

'Pull yourself together,' hissed Miss Amey.

'I'm sorry.' Beth wiped her eyes. 'It just hurts so much. I think I've done something really bad to it this time.'

'Don't be such a coward. I'll tell you the position once again, since your addled brain doesn't seem able to grasp it. You competed on three pieces of apparatus. We aren't allowed to put in the reserve now. Either you do your exercise, or we forfeit the mark. And that mark will make the difference between defeat and victory for us. Everyone else has finished. It's all up to you. Understand? Right. Put your weight on your leg. Go on. Up. How does that feel?'

Beth screamed. Her face went white, her blood might have all drained away. Miss Amey made a noise of impatience and left the room.

'Dr Kennedy, Beth wishes to try her beam exercise, but the knee is slightly painful. Could I have the anaesthetic spray? Thank you.'

Beth had thought that Miss Amey had given her up; that she was to have peace. Now here she was, back again. It was difficult to know just what was happening . . . the terrible pain shooting up and down her leg like fire, the voice screaming in her ear that she was a coward, she must go back out there. Out where? Oh, the match. What match?

'Will you *listen*! *Beth*! I've sprayed your knee with anaesthetic. The pain should go in a moment.' Beth looked down in surprise; why, so it had. How strange. Her leg had gone away.

'Beth! Pull yourself together! What do you think we pay you for? Get on your feet. Now get out there and for God's sake do that exercise. Do as much as you can. That bandage will hold your knee. Take the weight of the landing on your other leg. Now *go*!'

Beth wondered what the roaring noise was.

Jodie sat upright. Beth? It wasn't possible. Beth had just been carried off in agony. Oh, God, no. This was madness. No, not madness. Amey.

Beth stepped lightly up to the beam and leapt on, into a straddle position. The crowd were oddly hushed. The exercise progressed. Jodie moved closer. She saw that Beth was making slight adaptations, leaving certain things out, altering sequences of moves to favour her bad leg. It flowed smoothly; nobody not in the know would have realised. It was a masterly display of professionalism; never again would Amey be able to call Beth a gutless idiot. Jodie came nearer still, until she was able to see Beth's face – she expected grimaces, winces, even tears, but Beth looked serene and tranquil. It was like a miracle, as if a saint had touched and healed her.

The routine was almost over. Beth drew herself up, tensing for the end, readying herself for the Rostova. For a moment Jodie thought that she had decided not to do it. But then Beth gave a slight nod, almost as if she were saying – 'oh, yes, now I remember what I do' – and leapt, somersault, handspring, and then, as her knee gave way, the sickening crack of her head meeting the wood of the bar.

The Fortunate Few:
Tim Kennemore

Comment

We haven't yet got to the point at which gymnastics replaces football as the most popular spectator sport, complete with leagues and hooliganism, and perhaps we never shall. But you've probably noticed that some of the competitors in international events are very young, and they must have endured a lifetime of preparation rather like that described in this story. If we do reach the state of affairs described by Tim Kennemore, it will be a bad day for the young performers (retired at sixteen), because they will be under such a strict régime of diet and exercise and training that they'll never have time to enjoy being young. They will be deprived of something that can not be replaced.

Activities

– This fictional account seems, fortunately, far removed from Jackie's experience that you read about in 'Vaulting ambition' (Unit 5). Summarize the differences in a short paragraph of seventy-five words.
– You have heard that a friend of yours is about to enter professional sport. Write a letter of congratulations at being selected, but politely and tactfully point out some of the dangers.
– Write the newspaper article that might have appeared the day following Beth's disastrous fall.
– Watching sport – whether on television or by going in person – is a very popular pastime, more people watching than participating. Try to find out what enjoyment is gained from being a spectator by thinking about your enjoyment and by asking your parents and friends for their views.
– Imagine a conversation between Miss Amey, the coach, and the now hostile Jodie following this incident. Write it as a script.
– If you were the producer of this scene for television, what notes on the character of Miss Amey would you write for the department which chooses the actors?

Nuts and Bolts

Another grammatical term which might be used by teachers correcting your work is **clause**. This is a group of words containing a verb, usually forming part of a more important sentence. For example, in the first paragraph of the piece, 'as Beth did her exercise' is a clause; and in the next paragraph: 'If the Bush were to go through . . .'. Now find one or two clauses in the final paragraph of the passage.

Pronounce these words, syllable by syllable: vivacious, rhythmically, unacceptably, anaesthetic, professionalism. Note that in 'anaesthetic' *an* means 'not', so that the whole word means 'not perceiving' or 'not feeling'. Earlier in the piece there is another word beginning with **a** meaning 'not', about a third of the way through. Can you spot it?

Unit 30

Thinking about Riley

Alan lives in Belfast, torn by the near civil war between some Catholics and some Protestants; he plays in a Protestant band. After a fight with Fergus Riley, a Catholic boy of his own age, they find a revolver hidden in the cellar of a deserted house. They become friends, and return to the cellar to have another look at their find, intending to throw it in the river:

'That's a real gun all right,' Riley said, but although he tried to be he didn't sound too enthusiastic.

'You're right there,' I said, and I didn't sound all that bright, either. In fact I'll tell you the truth: I was wishing that I had never seen the thing. The gun was too big for us. We were just kids, after all, and the gun came from the world of men. Looking at it reminded me of the time when I was in the baths and went on to the top diving board. I was a good diver but I had never gone out on the board at that height, and when I got up there I was frightened out of my wits. I nearly fell off and in the end I had to sit down and crawl back to the tower. That's how I felt when I looked at the gun. It made me feel dizzy.

But when I picked it up it gave me the same funny feeling it had the first time I held it, as if it made you bigger and stronger, bigger and stronger than anyone else in the world. And when Riley had his turn it had the same effect on him. I could see it in his face. His eyes narrowed into little slits, like a pig, and his mouth turned down like a real gunfighter, and I wondered whether my face had looked the same.

'It's a revolver,' I said. 'That round thing's called the cylinder.' But I produced my knowledge without a flourish. Somehow it didn't seem knowledge worth having, like some of the really disgusting dirty stuff that Cather used to speak.

I had a look for the name and found it on the handle. It was a Webley, right enough. I pointed it out to Riley. He was very interested. 'Let's have a look.' He had a really good look, too. 'That's the gun the B Specials use. It's a British gun.'

I missed what he said. I heard it all right but I missed the significance of what he said, or how he said it. But it was getting dark. We could hardly see the gun any more so we put it back and climbed out of the cellar. We sloped off down to the little gate and asked a man the time. It was still only quarter to eight so we sat under a tree and Riley gave me a fag.

'Where are your bagpipes?' I asked.

'I dropped them off at the church,' he said. 'Where's your fife?'

'Here.' I took it out of my pocket. It didn't look very impressive.

'Why did you join the band?' Riley asked.

'I wanted to play the lambeg.' (big drum)

'Oh?' Riley's voice was soft but I knew what he was thinking.

'It was just because of the banging. There was nothing in it.'

Riley leaned on his side, his cigarette glowing in the dusk. 'No politics, hey?'

'Phew,' I spat, although not as neatly as Riley. 'I hear enough of that.'

'Do you go to church?' Riley asked.

'No.' I thought of the time I had gone into a Catholic church, and I wondered how Riley felt when he went. 'Do you go a lot?'

'Every Sunday, sometimes in the week, and confession on Friday night.'

I whistled. 'I wouldn't like to do that.' And I wouldn't have, either. Just the thought of it made me go red.

'It's nothing,' Riley said. 'There's ways of saying these things.' He flicked his cigarette away. 'Listen, where did you find out that stuff about the guns, the names?'

'My dad told me. He knows about guns. He was in the army.' I said that with a bit of pride in my voice but I was surprised when Riley casually answered.

'So was mine,' he said.

I was taken aback by that. Living where I did and with Jack forever booming in my ears you would have thought that a Catholic would have sooner jumped in the fire than join up.

'I mean the British Army,' I said.

'So do I,' Riley said. 'He was in the Royal Irish. What was your dad in?'

'The Lancashire Fusiliers.'

'Aye, there's a lot of Irish in that,' Riley said. 'But of course, your dad's not Irish, is he?'

I had to agree with that, although I didn't want to just then. It gave me a feeling I was being pushed out of something.

'Well.' Riley stretched his long legs. 'I've got to get to practice. I'll see you next Wednesday, OK?'

It was OK with me. 'Same time?' I asked.

'Yes.' Riley stood up. 'See you,' he said, and strode off into the dusk.

I sat under the tree for a minute or two finishing my fag and thinking about Riley. He had me guessing, I won't deny that. There didn't seem to be any difference between him and me. He was just a Belfast lad, his father had been in the army, he lived in a street like mine, and I was ready to bet that he liked a bit of modelling too. . . . It made me feel sad as the bell rang to clear the park and the kids ran from the swings, and the lights in the Orange Hall on our side, and the Catholic church on their side, gleamed through the dusk.

Under Goliath:
Peter Carter

Comment

Goliath was an enormous crane at the ship-yard in Belfast; Jack was a besotted Protestant supporter. Through his friendship with Fergus Riley, Alan gets involved in the suspicion and violence that destroy life in Northern Ireland. The story of Alan, which you can read in miniature here, gives us an idea of the insane and meaningless hatred between two opposing groups.

Activities

– Reread the last paragraph of the extract and underline the sentence that you think is the most important as a summary of Alan's thoughts.
– Very often young people see through the prejudices and suspicions of adults. Write a script in which you show both Alan and Fergus in their respective homes that evening commenting on their parents' views. You could write various scenes ending in a meeting with both sets of parents.
– What are your views about Northern Ireland and its future? Do you know any real facts? Find out as much as you can.
– Write a short story involving Alan and Fergus.
– Joan Lingard has written several books set in modern Belfast, including *The Twelfth Day of July, Across the Barricades,* and *Into Exile.*

Nuts and Bolts

Copy out from 'You're right there' to 'I was a good diver', making a full-stop at 'diver'. Put each of the sentences on a different line, mixing the order; it's helpful to number them for when you arrange them again.

Look back to Unit 25 and sort out the paragraph you jumbled.

Another technical term in grammar is **phrase**. It means a group of words that go together, without a verb. In the paragraph 'But when I . . .' one phrase is 'bigger and stronger than anyone else in the world'. Can you find two more phrases in the same paragraph, one of three words and one of four words?

'Effect' means 'result'. Link it with 'effective'.

Unit 31

Rat civilization

A research laboratory develops a highly intelligent strain of rats which can read. They escape and live in a large deserted house. Here one of them outlines their plan:

The reading we did! We knew very little about the world, you see, and we were curious. We learned about astronomy, about electricity, biology and mathematics, about music and art. I even read quite a few books of poetry and got to like it quite well.

But what I liked best was history. I read about the ancient Egyptians, the Greeks and Romans, and the Dark Ages when the old civilisations fell apart and the only people who could read and write were the monks. They lived apart in monasteries. They led the simplest kind of lives, and studied and wrote; they grew their own food, built their own houses and furniture. They even made their own tools and their own paper. Reading about them, I began getting some ideas of how we might live.

Most of the books were about people; we tried to find some about rats, but there wasn't much.

We did find a few things. There were two sets of encyclopedias that had sections on rats. From them we learned that we were about the most hated animals on earth, except perhaps snakes and germs.

That seemed strange to us, and unjust. Especially when we learned that some of our close cousins – squirrels, for instance, and rabbits – were well liked. But people think we spread diseases, and I suppose possibly we do, though never intentionally, and surely we never spread as many diseases as people themselves do.

Still, it seemed to us that the main reason we were hated must be that we always lived by stealing. From the earliest times, rats lived round the edges of human cities and farms, stowed away on men's ships, gnawed holes in their floors and stole their food. . .

Had we, then, no use at all in the world? One encyclopedia had a word of praise for us: 'The common rat is highly valued as an experimental animal in medical research due to his toughness, intelligence, versatility and biological similarity to man.' We knew quite a bit about that already.

But there was one book, written by a famous scientist, that had a chapter about rats. Millions of years ago rats seemed to be ahead of all the other animals, seemed to be making a civilisation of their own. They were well organised and built quite complicated villages in the fields. . . Their descendants today are the rats known as prairie dogs.

But somehow it didn't work out. The scientist thought maybe it was because the rats' lives were too easy; while the other animals (especially the monkeys) were living in the woods and getting tougher and smarter, the prairie dogs grew soft and lazy and made no more progress. . .

It was interesting to us that for a while, at least, the rats had been ahead. We wondered. If they had stayed ahead, if they had gone on and developed a real civilisation – what would it have been like? Would rats too have shed their tails and learned to walk erect? Would they have made tools? Probably, though we thought not so soon and not so many; a rat has a natural set of tools that monkeys lack; sharp, pointed teeth that never stop growing. Consider what the beavers can build with no tools but their rodent teeth.

Surely rats would have developed reading and writing, judging by the way we took to it. But what about machines? What about cars and aeroplanes? Maybe not aeroplanes. After all, monkeys, living in trees, must have felt a need to fly, must have envied the birds around them. Rats may not have had that instinct. . .

We thought and talked quite a bit about this, and we realised that a rat civilisation, if one ever did grow up, would not necessarily turn out to be anything like human civilisation. . . It was above ground, and that never felt quite natural to us.

So we decided that our new home should be underground, preferably, if we could find it, a cave. But where? We thought hard, and studied maps and atlases – there were plenty of those in the study. Finally, we reached some conclusions. To find a cave, we would have to go where there were mountains – there aren't many caves in flatlands. And for food, it would have to be near a town, or better, a farm.

So we wanted to find a farm, preferably a big one, with a big barn and silos full of grain, near the mountains. We studied the maps some more, and spotted this area as a good place to look. On the map, a big part of it was covered with the contour lines that show mountains, and across these were written the words, 'Thorn Mountains National Forest.' Beneath this, where the mountains turn to foothills, the map showed rolling country with quite a few roads but hardly any towns, which, we thought, ought to mean farmland.

We were right, as of course you know now. It took us two months of steady travelling to get to the Thorn Mountains National Forest, but we found it; we're under the edge of it right now. And there are plenty of caves, most of them never visited by people – because people aren't allowed to drive into a wilderness preserve. There aren't any roads in the forest, but only a few jeep trails used by rangers, and aeroplanes are not permitted to fly over it.

Mrs Frisby and the Rats of NIMH:
Robert C. O'Brien

Comment

We have included some units in this volume which take an unusual look at our civilization: 'The robots revolt' (Unit 23), 'Empty world' (Unit 28), and 'Rat civilization'. We believe it is right for us all to think carefully about our civilization in order, if we can, to improve our quality of life. By taking a vantage point outside our present circumstances, as in 'Rat Civilization', we are encouraged to examine those things we perhaps take for granted. Read the first two paragraphs again and you will see what we mean; the curiosity of the rats to learn and their desire to obtain models and 'ideas of how we might live'.

Activities

– One of these intelligent rats comes into your bedroom and scrutinizes your belongings. What report would the rat be able to make about the sort of character you are?
– What do you think you have gained from reading this excerpt? Note your thoughts.
– You find out about the rats setting up their community. Write a 200-word article for a newspaper. Make up a headline to accompany the article that will be sure to catch the attention.
– Read the book from which we have taken the extract and also *Z for Zachariah* by the same author.
– What were the Dark Ages?

Nuts and Bolts

In the first paragraph the items in a list are separated by **commas**. The comma is also used to mark off phrases, like 'Reading about them' at the end of the following paragraph.

We've already mentioned that the presence or absence of a comma can make a big difference to the meaning of a sentence. There is a vital one missing in this programme announcement:

Cantata No. 125 In Peace and Joy Shall I Depart with Doris Benson, contralto.

Pronounce carefully, syllable by syllable: mathematics, monasteries, intentionally, preferably. Notice that in the last word just listed the accent falls on the first syllable.

Unit 32

Girl meets boy

DEAR JILL, I met this wonderful boy at a disco and he asked me to go out with him. He's so handsome, and the way he smiles sends shivers down my spine. All my friends say he's no good and that I'm wasting my time with him, but I'm sure it's not so. Please tell me I'm doing the right thing. Miss G.P., Amortown, Kent.
DEAR MISS G.P., Looks aren't everything and you don't really know what this boy is like. Your friends may be jealous that he's asked you out of course. . .

Writing letters to magazines to seek advice isn't new. In *The Spectator* of over two hundred years ago, the writer Joseph Addison claims to have received the following letter from a young lady. Though no one would write quite like this nowadays – and there are a number of words and phrases that will seem a little strange to you – her 'problem' feels remarkably modern.

MR SPECTATOR, – Now, sir, the thing is this: Mr Shapely is the prettiest gentleman about town. He is very tall, but not too tall neither. He dances like an angel. His mouth is made I do not know how, but it is the prettiest that I ever saw in my life. He is always laughing, for he has an infinite deal of wit. If you did but see how he rolls his stockings! He has a thousand pretty fancies, and I am sure, if you saw him, you would like him. He is a very good scholar, and can talk Latin as fast as English. I wish you could but see him dance. Now you must understand poor Mr. Shapely has no estate; but how can he help that, you know? and yet my friends are so unreasonable as to be always teasing me about him, because he has no estate: but I am sure he has that that is better than an estate; for he is a good-natured, ingenious, modest, civil, tall, well-bred, handsome man, and I am obliged to him for his civilities ever since I saw him. I forgot to tell you that he has black eyes, and looks upon me now and then as if he had tears in them. And yet my friends are so unreasonable, that they would have me be uncivil to him. I have a good portion which they cannot hinder me of, and I shall be fourteen on the 29th day of August next, and am therefore willing to settle in the world as soon as I can, and so is Mr Shapely. But everybody I advise with here is poor Mr Shapely's enemy. I desire, therefore, you will give me your advice, for I know you are a wise man; and if you advise me well, I am resolved to follow it. I heartily wish you could see him dance, and am, Sir, your most humble servant,

B.D.

P.S He loves your *Spectators* mightily.

Courting has always had its different ways, as these two pieces show. First, four hundred years ago:

In our assemblies at plays in London, you shall see such heaving and shoving, such itching and shouldering to sit by women: such care for their garments, that they be not trod on: such pillows to their backs, that they take no hurt: such tickling, such toying, such smiling, such winking, and such manning them home, that it is a right comedy to mark their behaviour.

This is part of a modern sketch, called *A Many Splendoured Thing*, by Keith Waterhouse and Willis Hall. Joyce and Hettie are two usherettes standing at the back of a cinema watching a film. During their dialogue they never take their eyes from the screen.

JOYCE: I'm getting engaged on Monday.
HETTIE: Are you? What, to that ginger-headed feller?
JOYCE: Who? Jug-ears? (*With extreme scorn.*) No-o-o-o! No, it's another feller.
HETTIE: Lovely.
JOYCE: You know Hudson Verity's?
HETTIE: Yes?
JOYCE: Well, you know that book shop next to it?
HETTIE: Yes?
JOYCE: Well, you know the pub next door?
HETTIE: Yes?
JOYCE: Well, you know them petrol pumps just opposite?
HETTIE: Yes?
JOYCE: Well, he works there.
HETTIE: Very nice.
JOYCE: Do you know how I met him? He cracked me on the back of the neck with a two-inch bolt. He did! No, 'cause I always walk past there on my way to work. And I used to see this chap with crinkly hair. And every day when I walked past he used to flick nuts and bolts at me, so I knew he was interested. So I thought, I won't speak, I'll let him speak first – you don't want to cheapen yourself. Then one day I'm walking past and there's this big iron bolt comes whizzing through the air and catches me right on the back of the neck! I went straight up to him and I says: 'You big gormless pig.' So, of course we started going out together.
HETTIE: Oh?

Activities

– Write a letter, as if from Mr Spectator, in reply to B.D. Try to imitate her style of writing.
– Read about Joseph Addison and the early history of periodicals. You can find out from an encyclopaedia or from a dictionary of English literature.
– Make a list of words and phrases in the short piece written over two hundred years ago which suggest to you that it wasn't written in the twentieth century.
– What were your thoughts when you read Joyce's account of how her relationship started? What makes the conversation funny? Do you think this account is plausible? (Look up 'plausible' if you are unsure of its meaning.)
– Continue the conversation between Hettie and Joyce as you imagine it might have gone.

Nuts and Bolts

In the second paragraph 'Writing letters . . .' a pair of **dashes** is used to bring in an explanation or expansion of what has gone before. Make sure that you really do understand how the words between dashes fit in with what has just been written.

Find in the letter to the *Spectator* an example of **commas** separating the items in a list.

The paragraph 'Our assemblies' is one long list of items of behaviour, so that commas would not give the reader enough rest. Therefore **colons** are used to slow the reading up and provide pauses.

In the first three of Joyce's speeches several **apostrophes** are used. But one use differs from the other two. Do you see how?

When Joyce says 'them petrol pumps' she is making a mistake that is not acceptable in standard English. What is it? (Note the last sentence of Gerald Durrell's account at the end of *In a hole full of snakes*, Unit 27, where the same mistake occurs.)

Unit 33

Jiu-jitsu

On board a Japanese ship, the *Canada Maru*, Laurens van der Post is initiated into the art of jiu-jitsu by the captain, Mori. William Plomer is the author's companion:

Towards the end of our second afternoon on the *Canada Maru*, Mori decided that the time had come for play as well as culture, and he invited us to join him and the crew in their daily round of games. Plomer declined with some agitation. Forth I went like a scapegoat to sacrifice on a strange altar.

The games were staged on the after well-deck where the hatch covers had been removed and the hatches themselves been opened wide to the palest of blue afternoons, still and warm. On the deck, thick rice straw mats, beautifully woven and of a warm, glowing yellow, had been laid to cover the steel surface. We looked down on this stage, I dressed in tennis clothes, Plomer in brown corduroys, open-necked shirt and his large, dark, horn-rimmed glasses, possibly as much a shield against the eyes of an alien crowd, I used to think, as the light. Everyone in the ship who was not on watch was collecting in the alleyways connected to the deck, galley-hands, stokers, quarter-masters, stewards, sailors and officers. Too many of them for my liking were dressed in those coarse, off-white three-quarter length trousers and short kimonos tied round the waist with a girdle. I knew the sport from my reading at the time as jiu-jitsu, and had relished the mystique made of it in the *Boy's Own* paper to the point of acquiring a certain fearful respect for the extent to which the physically small and vulnerable, equipped with its skills, was able to master the uninitiated giants of muscle and brawn pitted against it. I was physically bigger than any potential opponents and considered myself in good condition. But there was a self-assurance in the eyes of the smaller men dressed for the occasion, and in the dismissive appraisal of me that they seemed to make depressingly quickly.

Plomer picked up some of the unease as well. He decided to stay where he was, out of reach of any more pressing invitations to participate. He watched what was to follow with the looks of a Christian compelled to bear witness to the martyrdom of a member of the faith in order to make a holiday for a Roman crowd massed in their Colosseum.

I went on my own to meet Mori down below. He was in high spirits and already dressed suitably; totally uninhibited by the temporary loss of uniform and badges of rank. He was on the easiest of terms with all the crew. It was indeed one of the nicest things about the moment, and a revelation of the underlying feeling that the Japanese seemed to have of all being united and equal in spirit through obedience to an order which seemed, on the surface, to be designed to divide them in as many social layers as a Neapolitan ice. I could have been walking into a family or clan gathering rather than into the assembly of a highly disciplined and differentiated crew.

One glance from Mori and my best tennis outfit was condemned. I had to strip off shift, trousers, shoes, socks and was made to put on the largest spare kimono uniform on the ship. In this I sat with the kind of inadequacy of a Victorian orphan most incongruously upon me; for something of amusement and a disagreeable relish of anticipation seemed to shine in the dark eyes of the massed *Canada Maru* clansmen, even though not a muscle or nerve twitched in their composed and courteous faces. By the time Mori had led me barefoot to those heavenly, soft mats, the rest of the gathering were squatting, legs crossed before them, upright and still, as if in imitation of Buddha, all round the open square of the hatchway. Once in the middle, Mori bowed to the watchers. I followed his example, awkwardly, with all the 'new boy' feelings of initiation which I thought I had left behind for good in my first months at school. He then addressed his audience in simple, forthright, unfaltering and appropriate words, all uttered in the voice of one born to command. He then turned and spoke to me in the same authoritative tones. He was, he declared, first of all going to teach me how to fall without doing myself injury in the process. He then said that, as in life, one had first to learn how to fall before one could learn how to get up and rise; first master the how of losing properly before one could be worthy of winning. So I was to be engaged in a sporting contest that was also the acting-out of a Japanese parable, and the well-deck was as much a place of religion as of fun and games.

After the exercises of correct falling and tumbling, Mori proceeded to throw me about with disdainful ease and an enjoyment which, at the climax, made me suspect that he had ceased to be the captain that either he or I knew. I was no longer the welcome guest. He briefly became all of Japan and I became all that had wounded and was still thwarting Japan in the west. But even then, magnanimous as he was at heart, he brought himself and me back into focus, putting an end to the throwing.

My turn ended, I joined the spectators, sitting among them trying hard also to be a credible version of Buddha. Mori, however, continued to have a few bouts with some of his sailors and demonstrated how he practised what he preached by falling with as great grace as the ease with which he had thrown me.

Yet Being Someone Other:
Laurens van der Post

Comment

This account of an incident on board ship gives an interesting insight into an aspect of Japanese life and culture. The 'daily round of games' has importance beyond that of merely keeping fit: all the crew are united and made equal by the games, no matter to which rank they belong; and the games teach a lesson about life, 'the acting-out of a Japanese parable', which prompts the author to suggest the games' almost religious significance.

Activities

– Imagine that someone asked you what sort of person Captain Mori was. Reread the extract, underlining the words and phrases which indicate his character, then write a seventy-word summary.
– Write the diary entry that the author might have written that evening. Would it have differed from William Plomer's very much?
– Look up any words used in the extract that are unfamiliar to you. Make sure you fit the meaning of each word in its context.
– 'The Contest.' Write a short story with this title. You may base it on a specific contest in which you took part.
– Have you ever been in a situation where you had 'first to learn how to fall' before you were able 'to get up and rise'? This does not necessarily have to be falling in a physical sense.
– Find out what a scapegoat is; who Buddha was; and where the original Colosseum was.

Nuts and Bolts

What are *italics* used for in this unit?

Look through all the words that are **hyphenated**, making sure, in each case, why a hyphen has been used.

Make a list of the **religious** words used by the author. If you find this difficult, you can find a clue to get you started at the end of *Comment*.

Unit 34

The whale

There was not a breath in the sky, glug-glug, glug-glug from the falling tide out through the Sound to the south, sea-birds in thousands on the water, porpoises diving in and out between each other on the edges of the tide, a patch of mackerel here and there, a white path of foam in the wake of the curragh, a bright shining fish taking a leap into the air with the fineness of the evening.

When we were about twenty yards from the Laoch reef I got a very nasty smell: 'Pooh, pooh!' I cried, for it was going through the back of my head.

'What ails you?'

'Och, don't you get the smell?'

I had hardly finished speaking when Michael and Padrig cried together: 'Pooh, pooh!'

At that moment I happened to glance out between me and Iveragh and about ten yards to the south I saw rings on the sea.

'The devil,' said I, 'what is that out there?'

Padrig gave a shout. 'Your soul to the devil, it's a whale, and it is from it we are getting the smell. Row, row as hard as you can and make for land.'

We pulled out, none of us speaking a word. There was nothing to be heard but the panting of the crew and the thud of the curragh leaping across a wave and the splash under her bow when she sent up a spurt of foam. We were pulling hard but had not gone far when the whale arose alongside the curragh – the biggest animal I ever saw, as long as a ship. You could see clearly its big blue gullet which could swallow three curraghs without any trouble. We were in great danger, out in the middle of the Great Sound, a couple of miles from land and that savage, ravenous, long-toothed monster up beside us, the way it had only to turn its head and swallow us up. I thought that at any moment we might be down in its belly. We were still pulling with all our strength, straining every sinew, the beast rolling along beside us, and from time to time giving us a side glance out of his two blue eyes.

'It will sink us if it moves across below the curragh,' said Padrig breathlessly. 'Row on, we are not far from land now, with the help of God.'

Our eyes and mouths were pouring sweat, our muscles bending with the strain, not a word spoken. I could hear the panting of the other two, the grating of the oars and the splashing of the beast through the water which kept sending spurts of foam into the curragh. And all the time the smell of its breath was affecting us. There was no escaping it.

'You had better not kill yourselves,' said Padrig, 'whatever it may do with us.'

He had scarcely spoken when the whale turned straight in towards the side of the boat.

'God have mercy on us, he has us now. Row! Row!'

'What about throwing out one of the dogs to it?' said I.

'Arra, devil, row, or it will get you instead of the dog.'

By this time we were only ten yards from Black Head. We began to take heart when we found ourselves inshore, scraping the limpets from the rocks in our haste. We rowed east till we went into the Cave of the Palm. The whale came no farther. We stopped. We were unable to speak. Our breath was gone and our mouths wide open trying to fill our lungs. Padrig caught hold of a bottle of water that was in the stern and took a long pull out of it.

'Oh, God of Virtues,' said he, 'what a hacking day! The likes of it never overtook me since I was born and God send it will not again. Arra, man,' said he to me, 'you were out of your mind that time, in the Great Sound, when you were for throwing the dog to the whale.'

'I wonder what it would have done if we had?' said Michael.

'You and the curragh would soon have been down its gullet.'

'Why do you say that, Padrig?'

'I will tell you. When the dog had pleased it, it would have been seeking another, though it would have only been a small morsel, and it would have set upon the curragh and swallowed us all.'

'What was in my mind,' said I, 'was that it would spend a nice while eating it and then we could escape.'

'Och, that beast wouldn't have known it wasn't a fly it had swallowed.'

The sun had sunk in the west, the stars were beginning to twinkle, wonderful colours spreading over the sky, a seal snoring here and there in the coves, rabbits over our heads among the clumps of thrift, sea-ravens standing on the rocks with their wings outspread.

Twenty Years A-Growing:
Maurice O'Sullivan

Comment

The author was born and bred in the Blasket Islands, which lie off the extreme south-west coast of Ireland. The people lived by fishing – for lobster in the summer and mackerel in the winter – growing potatoes in little patches of soil made of sand and seaweed, and keeping a few cows and sheep. They had to be tough and resourceful, doing most things for themselves, for there was no shop. They needed to be brave and skilful as well, when they managed their curraghs in the currents and rough seas of the Atlantic. Curraghs were light canoes made of tarred canvas stretched over a wicker frame; they could be carried by two men. Maurice and his friends were hauling up lobster pots when the whale shark chased them to safety.

The later part of his book tells how Maurice came to join the New Civic Guard (police) in Dublin. He wrote his story in Irish; what we read above is a translation. Little English was known in the islands, and the people did not read much. Their pastimes were singing, dancing, story-telling and conversation.

Activities

– How does Padrig differ from Michael and the narrator of the story?
– Find out about the different types of whale.
– What have men done to whales in the past hundred years or so; and what should now be done? (You may find it helpful to re-read the paragraph about the whaling industry in Unit 42 of Volume 2.)
– Men have always regarded whales with wonder and admiration. In the *Book of Jonah* in the Bible there is the famous fable about a great fish; and there is more in the *Book of Job*, Chapter 41, verses 1 to 7. Here God is telling Job how puny men are, compared with their creator; he mentions the great fish ('leviathan') as something far beyond their power to cope with. Read the two passages.
– Read Chapter 3, 'The Singing Whale', of Laurens van der Post's *Yet Being Someone Other*, the book from which we took the last unit, or one of: Frank Bullen's *The Cruise of the Cachalot*, Herman Melville's *Moby Dick* (we suggest a shortened version), F. D. Ommaney's *South Latitude*.

Nuts and Bolts

There is only one, not very important, verb in the first paragraph, because the writer's **aim** is not to record action, but to . . . ? Can you suggest what he is trying to do?

Why did the writer add the last little paragraph?

Unit 35

Absentmindedness in the choir

The church band had had little sleep for days, through playing at Christmas dances. On the Sunday after Christmas they were very tired, and the gallery they played in was unheated. So Nicholas took action to keep them warm:

He brought a gallon of hot brandy and beer, ready mixed, to church with him in the afternoon, and by keeping the jar well wrapped up in Timothy's bass-viol bag he kept it drinkably warm till they wanted it, which was just a thimbleful in the Absolution, and another after the Creed, and the remainder at the beginning o' the sermon. When they'd had the last pull they felt quite comfortable and warm, and as the sermon went on they fell asleep, every man jack of 'em; and there they slept on as sound as rocks.

'Twas a very dark afternoon, and by the end of the sermon all you could see was the parson's two candles in the pulpit. The sermon being ended at last, the parson gave out the evening hymn. But no choir set about sounding up the tune, and the people began to turn their heads to learn the reason why, and then Levi Limpet, a boy who sat in the gallery, nudged Timothy and Nicholas, and said, 'Begin! Begin!'

'Hey? what?' says Nicholas, starting up; and the church being so dark and his head so muddled he thought he was at the party they had played at all the night before, and away he went, bow and fiddle, at 'The Devil among the Tailors', the favourite jig of our neighbourhood at the time. The rest of the band, being in the same state of mind, followed their leader with all their strength. They poured out that there tune till the lower bass notes of the jig made the cobwebs in the roof shiver like ghosts; and then Nicholas, seeing nobody moved, shouted out (in his usual commanding way at dances when the folk didn't know the figures), 'Top couples cross hands! And when I make the fiddle squeak at the end, every man kiss his pardner under the mistletoe!'

The boy Levi was so frightened that he bolted down the gallery stairs and out homeward like lightning. The parson's hair fairly stood on end when he heard the evil tune raging through the church, and thinking the choir had gone crazy he said, 'Stop, stop, stop! What's this?' But they didn't hear him for the noise of their own playing, and the more he called the louder they played.

Then the folks came out of their pews, saying 'What do they mean by such wickedness! We shall be consumed like Sodom and Gomorrah!'

Then the squire came out of his pew lined with green baize, where lots of lords and ladies visiting at the house were worshipping along with him, and went and stood in front of the gallery, and shook his fist in the musicians' faces, saying, 'What! In this reverent edifice! What!'

And at last they heard him through their playing, and stopped.

'Never such an insulting disgraceful thing, never!' says the squire, who couldn't rule his passion.

'Never!' says the parson, who had come down and stood beside him.

'Not if the angels of Heaven,' says the squire (he was a wickedish man, the squire was, though now for once he happened to be on the Lord's side) – 'not if the angels of Heaven come down,' he says, 'shall one of you villainous players ever sound a note in this church again; for the insult to me, and my family, and my visitors, and God Almighty, that you've perpetrated this afternoon!'

Then the unfortunate church band came to their senses, and remembered where they were; and 'twas a sight to see Nicholas Pudding come and Timothy Thomas and John Biles creep down the gallery stairs with their fiddles under their arms, and poor Daniel Hornhead with his serpent, and Robert Dowdle with his clarionet, all looking as little as ninepins; and out they went. The parson might have forgiven 'em when he learned the truth of it, but the squire would not. That very week he sent for a barrel-organ that would play two-and twenty new psalm-tunes, so exact and particular, that however sinful inclined you were, you could play nothing but psalm-tunes whatsoever. He had a really respectable man to turn the winch, as I said, and the old players played no more.

Life's Little Ironies:
Thomas Hardy

Comment

Over a hundred years ago music in country churches was often provided by a band of five or six musicians, who usually played in a gallery at the back of the church. On the dark winter afternoon of Hardy's story the body of the church was heated by a stove, but there was no warmth in the gallery; nor was there any lighting apart from candles, and perhaps an oil lamp or two when night fell. In those days there was no television and no tape recorders and no public transport, so villages had to make their own entertainment; and naturally the church band was called on to play at dances, especially at Christmas.

The serpent was a wind instrument, with turns that made it look like a thick-bodied snake. Barrel-organs were so-called because they were fitted with big cylindrical records with notches; they worked like large-scale musical boxes. The Absolution and the Creed are part of the morning and evening services in the Church of England. According to the *Book of*

Genesis, Sodom and Gomorrah were towns that were burned up because they had offended God.

Activities

– What was the Squire's opinion of himself and his position in the parish? And what did Hardy think of him?
– Invent a headline for a local newspaper article about the event.
– Can you invent a somewhat similar situation for today, when something goes comically wrong? Perhaps someone who has come to open a new building or distribute prizes has had rather a good lunch, and thinks he is at a company meeting or some quite different event – and delivers the wrong speech.
– Write the letter the parson might have written the next day to a colleague in a neighbouring parish.
– See if a nearby museum has a serpent. If not, try to find a book containing an illustration.
– Read Hardy's *Under the Greenwood Tree* – and find out more about church bands, galleries and the noise made by a serpent.

Nuts and Bolts

This is a story supposed to have been told to the passengers in a carrier's van on its way back from market to the village. Can you find some signs that it was a story told aloud?

Some of the **dialect** has been turned into present-day English for ease of reading. Dialects are local languages, but they are in no way inferior to standard English; in fact they are often livelier.

Unit 36

No place to go to

In the middle of the last century a journalist interviewed scores of destitute people in London. The boy of sixteen interviewed here slept rough in London in the hope of getting to sea:

I got crusts, but I can hardly tell how I lived. One night I was sleeping under a railway arch, somewhere about Bishopsgate Street, and a policeman came and asked what I was up to. I told him I had no place to go to, so he said I must go along with him. In the morning he took me and four or five others to a house in a big street. I don't know where; and a man – a magistrate, I suppose he was – heard what the policeman had to say, and he said there was always a lot of young lads there about the arches, young thieves, that gave him a great deal of trouble, and that I was associated with them. I declare that I didn't know any of the other boys, nor any boys in London – not a soul; and I was under the arch by myself, and only that night. I never saw the policeman himself before that, as I know of. I got fourteen days of it, and they took me in an omnibus, but I don't know to what prison. I was committed for being a rogue and something else. I didn't very well hear what other things I was, but 'rogue' I know was one. They were very strict in prison, and I wasn't allowed to speak. I was put to oakum some days, and others on a wheel. That's the only time I ever was in prison, and I hope it will always be the only one. Something may turn up – there's nobody knows.

When I was turned out I hadn't a farthing given me. And so I was again in the streets, without knowing a creature, and without a farthing in my pocket, and nothing to get one with but my tongue. I set off that day for the country. I didn't try to get a ship for I didn't know where to go to ask, and I had got ragged, and they wouldn't hear me out if I asked any people about the bridges. I took the first road that offered, and it got me to Greenwich. I couldn't still think of going back home. I would if I had had clothes, but they were rags, and I had no shoes but a pair of old slippers. I was sometimes sorry I left home, but then I got used to travelling, and to beg a bit in the villages. I had no regular mate to travel with, and no sweetheart. I slept in the unions whenever I could get in – that's in the country. I didn't never sleep in the London workhouses till afterwards. In some places there were as many as forty in the casual wards, men, women, and children; in some, only two or three. There used to be part boys, like myself, but far more bigger than I was; they were generally from eighteen to twenty-three; London chaps chiefly, I believe.

They were a regularly jolly lot. They used to sing and dance a part of the nights and mornings in the wards, and I got to sing and dance with them. We were all in a mess; there was no better or no worse among us. We used to sing comic and sentimental songs, both. I used to sing 'Tom Elliott', that's a sea song, for I hankered about the sea, and 'I'm Afloat'. I hardly know any but sea-songs. Many used to sing indecent songs; they're impudent blackguards. They used to sell these songs among the others, but I never sold any of them, and I never had any, though I know some, from hearing them often. We told stories sometimes; romantic tales, some; other blackguard tales; and others about thieving and roguery; not so much about what they'd done themselves, as about some big thief that was very clever at stealing, and could trick anybody. Not stories such as Dick Turpin or Jack Sheppard, or things that's in history, but inventions.

Sometimes there was fighting in the casual wards. Sometimes I was in it, I was like the rest. We jawed each other often, calling names, and coming to fight at last. At Romsey a lot of young fellows broke all the windows they could get at, because they were too late to be admitted. They broke them from the outside. We couldn't get at them from inside. I've carried on begging, and going from union to union to sleep, until now. Once I got work in Northampton with a drover. I kept working when he'd a job, from August last to the week before Christmas.

I always tried to get a ship in a seaport, but I couldn't. I've been to Portsmouth, Plymouth, Bristol, Southampton, Ipswich, Liverpool, Brighton, Dover, Shoreham, Hastings, and all through Lincolnshire, Nottinghamshire, Cambridgeshire and Suffolk – not in Norfolk – they won't let you go there. I don't know why. All the time I used to meet boys like myself, but mostly bigger and older; plenty of them could read and write, some were gentlemen's sons, they said. Some had their young women with them that they'd taken up with, but I never was much with them. I often wished I was at home again, and do now, but I can't think of going back in these rags; and I don't know if my father's dead or alive (his voice trembled), but I'd like to be there and have it over. I can't face meeting them in these rags, and I've seldom had better, I make so little money. I'm unhappy at times, but I get over it better than I used, as I get accustomed to this life. I never heard anything about home since I left. I have applied at the Marine Society here, but it's no use. If I could only get to sea, I'd be happy; and I'd be happy if I could get home, and would, but for the reasons I've told you.'

London Labour and the London Poor:
Henry Mayhew

Comment

Everything about this piece makes it sound as if it all happened a long time ago – the arrest, the offence, the punishment and other examples that you will have thought of. Many other things have gone, including the 'unions' or workhouses, where there were casual wards, in which tramps could put up for the night. But there is one evil we have not put right, and that is the plight of the homeless in London. They include many teenagers, attracted by the chance of getting a job of which there is no hope in their home town. They have much in common with the boy who tells his story here.

Activities

– Make some notes of the boy's account to help you remember the details, then talk to a parent or friend about the boy and his plight.

– Write a script for a short sketch involving the boy and two or three others, set in one of the 'wards' one evening.

– Dip into the book from which we have taken the account; you will find some interesting characters.

– Write the report the policeman might have given to the magistrate.

– The sea has always provided an attraction. Read the opening chapter of Joseph Conrad's *Lord Jim*. Jim has an idea of himself as a hero and a great sailor.

– What did a drover do? And what were 'oakum' and the 'wheel'? Who was Dick Turpin?

Nuts and Bolts

Write out the first six sentences (as far as 'home') of the paragraph 'When I was turned out'. Mix up the order, and write them on separate lines.

Look back to Unit 30 and sort out your sentences from the jumbled paragraph.

Note the spelling of 'committed' and 'rogue', and the plural 'thieves' (see Unit 16).

Unit 37

Around the world on pocket money

Anyone who starts to collect stamps will soon realise the enormity of the field and the need, eventually, for some sort of specialisation. Even to keep up with the new stamps issued in the world each year – some 6000 of them – is a virtual impossibility.

But the young collector can derive considerable pleasure and interest from spreading the net as wide as possible, discovering, for instance, just how many countries he or she can find examples from. Since it is estimated that some 300 nations and territories currently issue stamps, there is plenty of scope.

Adopting the global approach is also a painless way of absorbing history and geography. Stamps provide a useful historical record, reflecting changes in name and status and often depicting memorable events. The development of postwar Africa, for example, can be very effectively illustrated through a stamp collection.

As for geography, much of the fascination of stamps for the beginner is discovering their place of origin. This is by no means always obvious, particularly when dealing with countries that no longer exist or have unfamiliar alphabets or scripts. For that matter, how many collectors overseas have puzzled over British stamps, which do not carry the name of the country?

Stamps are easy enough to come by, whether simply taken off letters, cadged from friends and relatives or bought in made-up packets. Packs can be found in most newsagents but the quality varies and it is probably better to pay a little more at a recognised dealer. A pack of 500 'all different' world stamps can be had for between £3 and £4 and makes an excellent start.

From then on it is a matter of extending the collection according to taste and interest, filling in gaps and, perhaps, starting to concentrate on certain areas. Joining a stamp club provides a chance not only to make contact with fellow collectors but also to swell your collection through swaps. There are fewer stamp clubs in schools than there used to be but some adult clubs have a junior section. The local public library should be able to provide details.

A good source of foreign stamps is an overseas pen friend. You can exchange the latest issues from your countries. The stamp club may be able to help with finding suitable correspondents or you could respond to advertisements in stamp magazines.

A look at dealers' prices for stamps, used and unused, will offer a guide to what it is feasible to collect, since most collectors must operate within a budget. As with any hobby, once you progress beyond a fairly elementary stage money becomes an important consideration and choices have to be made.

One course is to become what in stamp circles is called a 'thematic' collector. Having obtained a general introduction to the subject by covering the whole field, you decide on an approach that is more limited though by no means less rewarding.

I have an acquaintance who devotes many of his spare hours to assembling every stamp he can lay hands on that bears the distinctive features of his hero, General de Gaulle. One day, surely, it will be a definitive collection. Already it is a matter of pride and an absorbing interest.

The Times:
Peter Waymark

Comment

Though postal systems had existed in various parts of the world for centuries, it was through the strenuous efforts of one man, Rowland Hill, that we owe the modern postage stamp. Supported by public opinion, Hill managed to establish the cheap adhesive stamp, the Penny Black, in 1840.

The invention proved especially important for ordinary men and women in that, for the first time in history, they were able to communicate with others from whom they were separated; parents could keep in touch with sons who had gone overseas to seek their fortunes. But, as a cheap and efficient mode of communication, it also proved its success with the world of business. The financial reward it brought to the Post Office, who had been most reluctant to have anything to do with it, ensured its continuation. It established a standard to which other countries tried to attain.

General de Gaulle

Activities

– You have recently become interested in philately and mention your interest to some friends, hoping to acquire some stamps from them; but one of your friends says it's a useless hobby. Using only the information in the article, write a letter to your friend explaining what is interesting and worthwhile.
– Do you collect matchbox labels, dolls in national costume, unusual bottles, coins, shells, records, or anything else? If so, write an article or report of a similar nature to the article on stamps. You could send it to the editor of your local newspaper.
– 'The Find.' Write a story – based on experience, if possible – about a discovery. It might be a fossil or a video game that every shop had stocked, but had 'just sold the last one', until. . .
– It is unusual to find poems about stamps. Here is one for you to read:

Stamp collection

Dust has engrained these blue-bound albums,
spines bent, cheap pages staining into brown;
and all their scraps of coloured paper
seem forlorn – like messages themselves
but gone astray, as if they were washed up
from desert islands, but too late, or
no one understood the message to bring help.
They are a catalogue of past pretensions,
lost identities, failed bids for freedom.

What maps today show Lebuan, or Oubangui-Chari,
Ifni or Manchukuo? Forgotten peoples leave
an imprint here: 'Jubaland, in East Africa,
ceded to Italy by Britain – 1924'. Does
anyone remember why? Or this sad tale:
'Ingermanland, a country in the north of Russia,
east of the Finnish border; it rebelled
in 1920 and declared its independence;
issued stamps. The revolt was soon suppressed.'

You could construct a history of Germany
from stamps: contested towns and regions
issuing their own, like desperate flags –
Danzig, Sudeten, Alsace-Lorraine, the Saar;
modest denominations of the Weimar years
all over-stamped in hundreds, thousands,
millions of marks. Bismarck, the Kaiser,
Hitler, each, for a set or two, appear and
then give way to post-war self-effacement.

Part of the magic was in mastering names –
Magyar Kir Posta, Suomi, Greece – much
easier to distinguish than the small square
portraits of dull heroes, whiskered kings.
All this was back before the days when
Arab emirates, Pacific atolls, barely
the size of postage stamps themselves,
started to print great gaudy triangles
with butterflies, fast cars and astronauts.

I never learnt about their proper care
or value, never pored over Stanley Gibbons'
heavy tomes, I just stuck stamps in books –
something a schoolboy was supposed to do.
This quirky residue that I now find, a mix
of rare and, mostly, commonplace – some
pages full, whole countries blank – looks
like a kind of practice for the pigeon-holing
of that tide of circumstances which daily living
posts through the sorting-office of the mind.

Tony Lucas

Nuts and Bolts

As the piece on pocket money was written for publication in a newspaper, the **paragraphs** tend to be short – to enable them to be easily taken in by readers in a hurry. But in a book a string of short paragraphs tends to give an effect of breathlessness. See if you can find two paragraphs which could well be joined; then see if there are any more which could receive the same treatment. There is no right or wrong here; it is your opinion that is wanted.

'Enormity' is intended by the writer to mean 'great size'. But our biggest dictionary says it is a mistake to use the word in this way. What does your dictionary say?

Unit 38

Ballads

As you watch *Top of the Pops* on television or go to a disco, you are probably unaware that the pop singer, playing his guitar and singing of love and sorrow, is the modern counterpart of a tradition going back over many centuries. The old ballads (the word itself being connected with singing and dancing) told simple stories of magic, adventure, love, murder, local and national history. The legends and stories of Robin Hood provided material for many.

We have no idea who wrote the old ballads; the authorship must remain a tantalizing mystery. And strictly speaking, they weren't written down anyway. It would be better to say that they were composed, probably by a single author, and then altered and adapted as they were passed on from generation to generation by word of mouth. It was many, many years later that the ballads were written down. How did they survive for so long? They were *memorable*: first, because the stories were enjoyable and satisfied those who knew them; and secondly, because ballads have a strong rhythm – hardly surprising, given their musical origins – and generally have the second and fourth lines rhyming. (See Volume 2, Unit 14 'Everyday poetry', for more information.)

Billy Bragg

Ballads use simple language and set the scene economically, with the minimum of description, telling the story dramatically through dialogue and action. Here is a little-known ballad – a simple love story:

The royal fisherman

As I walked out one May morning,
When May was all in bloom,
O there I spied a bold fisherman,
Come fishing all alone.

I said to this bold fisherman,
'How come you fishing here?'
'I'm fishing for your own sweet sake
All down the river clear.'

He drove his boat towards the side,
Which was his full intent,
Then he laid hold of her lily-white hand
And down the stream they went.

Then he pulled off his morning gown
And threw it over the sea,
And there she spied three robes of gold
All hanging down his knee.

Then on her bended knees she fell:
'Pray, sir, pardon me
For calling you a fisherman
And a rover down the sea.'

'Rise up, rise up, my pretty fair maid,
Don't mention that to me,
For not one word that you have spoke
Has the least offended me.

'Then we'll go to my father's hall,
And married we shall be,
And you shall have your fisherman
To row you on the sea.'

Then they went to his father's house,
And married now they be;
And now she's got her fisherman
To row her down the sea.

Notice how simply the story unfolds. Details are sparse, though sufficient information is given for us to visualize the scene and feel the girl's shock at realizing that the fisherman is a prince.

Love of a rather different kind is the subject of a modern ballad by the poet B. S. Johnson.

Song of the Wagondriver

My first love was the ten-ton truck
they gave me when I started,
and though she played the bitch with me
I grieved when we were parted.

Since then I've had a dozen more,
the wound was quick to heal,
and now it's easier to say
I'm married to my wheel.

I've trunked it north, I've trunked it south,
on wagons good and bad,
but none were ever really like
the first I ever had.

The life is hard, the hours are long,
sometimes I cease to feel,
but I go on, for it seems to me
I'm married to my wheel.

Often I think of my home and kids,
out on the road at night,
and think of taking a local job
provided the money's right.

Two nights a week I see my wife,
and eat a decent meal,
but otherwise, for all my life,
I'm married to my wheel.

In Shakespeare's *The Winter's Tale*, the country people are eager for stories from the ballads being sold by a rogue. According to the rogue, Autolycus, one ballad is about

> 'a fish that appeared upon the coast on Wednesday the fourscore of April, forty thousand fathom above water, and sung this ballad against the hard hearts of maids. It was thought she was a woman, and was turn'd into a cold fish.'

When asked if this 'tall' story is true, he cheekily replies:

> 'Five justices' hands at it; and witnesses more than my pack will hold.'

A likely story, indeed!

Activities

– Try to write one or two ballads, taking your subjects from items in the newspaper, news items being exactly what the early ballad makers would have chosen. Here are three such examples from a newspaper: a family rescued from a sinking cabin cruiser in the English Channel; an elderly couple celebrating their golden wedding; a boy who cycles from Land's End to John o' Groats to raise money for charity.
– There are hundreds and hundreds of ballads that you could read. These are famous old ballads that you ought to be able to find fairly easily: *Sir Patrick Spens, The Twa Corbies, The Unquiet Grave, The Wife of Usher's Well, Thomas Rymer, Edward, Edward.*
– Find out more about ballads from a dictionary of English literature or by reading the introduction to one of the several ballad anthologies available.

Nuts and Bolts

Think of the **adjectives** from which these words are formed: probably, generally, economically, dramatically, simply; and note how the **adverbs** are made. Adjectives ending in **-ic** are often lengthened to make an adverb: 'frantic' becomes 'frantically'. You **can** say 'franticly', but it is much easier to say 'frantically'. Think of another **-ic** word and see how it works.

Unit 39

The breadwinner

The parents of a boy of fourteen were waiting for him to come home with his first week's wages.

The mother had laid the table and was cutting some slices of bread and butter for tea. She was a little woman with a pinched face and a spare body, dressed in a blouse and skirt, the front of the skirt covered with a starched white apron. She looked tired and frequently sighed heavily.

The father, sprawling inelegantly in an old armchair by the fireside, legs outstretched, was little too. He had watery blue eyes and a heavy brown moustache, which he sucked occasionally.

These people were plainly poor, for the room, though clean, was meanly furnished, and the thick pieces of bread and butter were the only food on the table.

As she prepared the meal, the woman from time to time looked contemptuously at her husband. He ignored her, raising his eyebrows, humming, or tapping his teeth now and then with his finger-nails, making a pretence of being profoundly bored.

'You'll keep your hands off the money,' said the woman, obviously repeating something that she had already said several times before. 'I know what'll happen to it if you get hold of it. He'll give it to me. It'll pay the rent and buy us a bit of food, and not go into the till at the nearest public-house.'

'You shut your mouth,' said the man, quietly.

'I'll not shut my mouth!' cried the woman, in a quick burst of anger. 'Why should I shut my mouth? You've been boss here for long enough. I put up with it when you were bringing money into the house, but I'll not put up with it now. You're nobody here. Understand? *Nobody*. *I'm* boss and he'll hand the money to me!'

'We'll see about that,' said the man, leisurely poking the fire.

Nothing more was said for about five minutes.

Then the boy came in. He did not look older than ten or eleven years. He looked absurd in long trousers. The whites of his eyes against his black face gave him a startled expression.

The father got to his feet.

'Where's the money?' he demanded.

The boy looked from one to the other. He was afraid of his father. He licked his pale lips.

'Come on now,' said the man. 'Where's the money?'

'Don't give it to him,' said the woman. 'Don't give it to him, Billy. Give it to me.'

The father advanced on the boy, his teeth showing in a snarl under his big moustache.

'Where's that money?' he almost whispered.

The boy looked him straight in the eyes.

'I lost it,' he said.

'You – *what*?' cried his father.

'I lost it,' the boy repeated.

The man began to shout and wave his hands about.

'Lost it! *Lost* it! What are you talking about? How could you lose it?'

'It was in a packet,' said the boy, 'a little envelope. I lost it.'

'Where did you lose it?'

'I don't know. I must have dropped it in the street.'

'Did you go back and look for it?'

The boy nodded. 'I couldn't find it,' he said.

The man made a noise in his throat, half grunt, half moan – the sort of noise that an animal would make.

'So you lost it, did you?' he said. He stepped back a couple of paces and took off his belt – a wide, thick belt with a heavy brass buckle. 'Come here,' he said.

The boy, biting his lower lip so as to keep back the tears, advanced, and the man raised his arm. The woman, motionless until that moment, leapt forward and seized it. Her husband, finding strength in his blind rage, pushed her aside easily. He brought the belt down on the boy's back. He beat him unmercifully about the body and legs. The boy sank to the floor, but did not cry out.

When the man had spent himself, he put on the belt and pulled the boy to his feet.

'Now you'll get off to bed,' he said.

'The lad wants some food,' said the woman.

'He'll go to bed. Go and wash yourself.'

Without a word the boy went into the scullery and washed his hands and face. When he had done this he went straight upstairs.

The man sat down at the table, ate some bread and butter and drank two cups of tea. The woman ate nothing. She sat opposite him, never taking her eyes from his face, looking with hatred at him. Just as before, he took no notice of her, ignored her, behaved as if she were not there at all.

When he had finished the meal he went out.

Immediately he had shut the door the woman jumped to her feet and ran upstairs to the boy's room.

He was sobbing bitterly, his face buried in the pillow. She sat on the edge of the bed and put her arms about him, pressed him close to her breast, ran her fingers through his disordered hair, whispered

endearments, consoling him. He let her do this, finding comfort in her caresses, relief in his own tears.

After a while his weeping ceased. He raised his head and smiled at her, his wet eyes bright. Then he put his hand under the pillow and withdrew a small dirty envelope.

'Here's the money,' he whispered.

She took the envelope and opened it and pulled out a long strip of paper with some figures on it – a ten shilling note and a sixpence.

The Breadwinner: Leslie Halward

Comment

This story needs no explanation. It tells us far more than is actually stated; for example we can learn that the father must have behaved very badly for a long time, for things to have got as bad as they are here.

One point is noticeable. Only the boy is given a name; this underlines the fact that he is the most important person in the tale. The title also makes this clear.

Unit 39 continued

Activities

– As Billy does well at his job, he earns more. He takes his mother on a shopping expedition to buy her, as a surprise, something she very much wants. Describe the expedition.

– It sometimes happens that bad men and women improve with the years, as they wake up and perhaps realize how dependent they are on others. Describe how this might happen with Billy's father.

– Write a short story ending with the words: 'After that there was no more interference from Dad.'

– A neighbour tells the NSPCC that Billy is being ill-treated by his father. An inspector calls to investigate. Write down the dialogue that takes place between the man and the visitor.

– Many people would probably agree that Billy was right to tell his father a lie. Have a discussion with your friends about telling lies. Is lying ever justified? Should we encourage children to believe in Father Christmas, for example? Are there lies you have regretted telling?

– Read *Gumble's Yard* by John Rowe Townsend and *The Railway Children* by E. Nesbit. Both are about families that manage for a time to get on without their father.

Nuts and Bolts

This story makes a deep impression on the reader because it is so simply told; there is not a word more than is needed, and every word pulls its weight. Look at the adjectives and adverbs in the first three paragraphs, and see how effective they are.

Find the paragraph 'The boy . . .' and write out its six sentences, in jumbled order, on separate lines.

Look back to Unit 36 and sort out the paragraph you jumbled.

In Comment you'll see the word 'noticeable', obviously made up from 'notice' and '-able'. Usually when **-able** is added to a word ending in **e**, the **e** is dropped: measure, measurable. 'Noticeable' keeps its **e**, because **c** like **g** can be pronounced hard or soft: can, ice; gun, gin. The e is kept to show that the **c** is soft. Contrast it with 'practicable'. And compare 'navigable' with 'manageable', where the **e** keeps the **g** soft. These words do not usually cause trouble; this note is given by way of explanation.

Unit 40

The supersonic era begins

The following article appeared on 22 January 1976 in *The Times*. It was written in Bahrain by Arthur Reed, Air Correspondent:

In a meticulously timed operation with Air France, which put dozens of subsonic airlines behind schedule, British Airways launched the supersonic era of civil aviation today.

Their Concorde Alpha Alpha touched down here from London in three hours and 37 minutes, clipping two hours and 43 minutes off the normal journey time, and arriving 19 minutes before schedule.

The British Airways Concorde appeared at the end of the runway at Heathrow Airport, London, five minutes before its scheduled take-off time which was arranged to coincide exactly with the take off of the first Air France passenger service from Charles de Gaulle airport, Paris, some 250 miles away. Captain Norman Todd, aged 50, the commander of the 1350 mph airliner, kept Alpha Alpha sitting on the ground while a queue of subsonic jumbo jets built up behind.

Both Pan American and Trans World, two United States airlines which originally took out options to buy Concordes and then cancelled them, were among those who had to wait.

Heathrow air traffic control, who were in contact with their French opposite numbers, gave a count-down at precisely the same moment to both Captain Todd and Captain Pierre Chanoine, in command of the French Concorde bound for Rio de Janeiro by way of Dakar, West Africa. Both commanders opened the throttles and the civil supersonic era was born.

The British Airways Concorde roared down the runway for 35 seconds, watched by thousands of spectators crowding the rails at the airport, before it was airborne at 11.40 a.m. The engines were throttled back briefly to reduce the impact of the noise on the communities living at the end of the runway, and then Concorde was climbing away at an angle of 25 degrees to its subsonic cruising height across Europe of 25 000 feet.

Over Paris, Captain Todd exchanged good wishes with Captain Chanoine over the radio.

One hour and 20 minutes later, over the northern end of the Adriatic, the 100 passengers on board felt a distinct surge of power as the airliner was accelerated through the sound barrier. Over the cabin address system, Captain Todd announced: 'Ladies and gentlemen, we are now supersonic.'

Twenty minutes later the digital display in the passenger cabin indicated that we were flying at twice the speed of sound to the accompaniment of a round of applause from the 30 passengers who had paid the £676.20 round trip fare and the 70 invited guests. Unfortunately the display in the rear cabin, where the

Unit 40 continued

guest of honour, the Duke of Kent, was seated, stuck at Mach 0.7 (about 460 mph) and no amount of banging of it by passengers could get it working again.

Lunch of smoked salmon, breast of duck and fresh strawberries was served as the Concorde boomed its way over the islands of Crete and Cyprus, then across Lebanon and Syria. Thirty minutes before landing, reverse thrust was applied in flight and we began to descend from our cruising height of 12 miles into Bahrain.

The flight was enriched by the presence on board of a gentleman from Trowbridge, Wiltshire, dressed overall in a fancy dress of white and purple and with his face painted silver. Mr Bob Ingham, aged 50, the manager of a plant hire company, said his outfit represented the age of Aquarius. He changed into it in a lavatory at the airport and then had some trouble in convincing the strict security guard that he was a bona fide passenger.

Comment

The article was reprinted in *The Times* of 22 January 1985 as part of a series commemorating the two hundred years of the newspaper's history. In the first edition of the paper, then called *The Daily Universal Register*, on 1 January 1785, the following appeared – about a mode of transport very different from Concorde:

For NICE, GENOA, and LEGHORN
(With Liberty to touch at One Port in the Channel,)
The N A N C Y.
THOMAS WHITE, Commander
BURTHEN 160 Tons; Guns and Men answerable.
Lying off the Tower, and will absolutely depart on Saturday the 8th instant.

The said Commander to be spoken with every morning at Sam's Coffee-house, near the Custom-house; at Will's Coffee-house, in Cornhill; and at Exchange hours on the French and Italian Walk, or WILLIAM ELYARD, for the said Commander,
No. 16 Savage-Gardens.

Activities

– Prepare a set of questions that you would like to ask Captain Todd if you were given the opportunity to interview him.
– Re-read the fourth paragraph concerning Pan American and Trans World airlines and write the newspaper article that might have appeared in the United States about the first two Concordes. Would the report be as enthusiastic and full? What would have been omitted?
– In the early days of air travel, the argument was put forward that, if he had intended us to fly, God would have given us wings. How would you reply to such a comment in the days of supersonic flight?
– What is Mach?
– Look in an atlas to trace the routes travelled by the two planes.

Nuts and Bolts

The two pieces from *The Times* quoted above had very different aims. What were they?

Adverbs again. In the sentence 'They co-operated together', the word 'together' is not wanted, because the **co** of 'co-operate' already means 'together'. In this piece 'take-off was arranged to coincide exactly . . .'. Is 'exactly' really needed?

English likes **metaphors**. Notice 'launched' and 'clipping' near the beginning. 'Launch' means to push a boat into the water, 'clip' means to cut off. No shoving or cutting was done here, so the use of the two words is metaphorical.

Unit 41

Mr Brunswick and I

Charles's music teacher leaves the district, so he goes to Mr Brunswick, a large untidy man. But they do not get on:

Old Baggypants was a fairly well-known man of the village. Once a year he gave a recital in the parish church, once a year we were invited to go along, and once a year we politely thought up some excuse for not going. It wasn't that we disliked Brunswick – on the contrary, my parents at least thought he was a dear old lad – but we knew what to expect if we went. There would be Nocturnes by Chopin, Rhapsodies by Liszt and Fugues by Bach, and those really were not our kinds of music – we would prefer to hear something less heavy and less boring.

By now I had come to think of everything associated with Mr Brunswick as heavy and boring – his music, his clothes, his house and his personality. Some days I would get absolutely sick and tired of music and would vow never ever to touch the keys again. My parents felt the time had come for a change.

So for the second time I had a change of tutors, and for the second time I was disappointed with what I got. This new fellow was also a Beethoven/Bach/Chopin fan (but much worse) and he was another of the music merchants who love scales etc. He talked too much, but he was also too full of his own importance. It may have been his job to criticise my playing, but it went further than that. 'Your mother's over-ambitious and your father's only interested in you because he has to pay the bill,' was one of his creepier comments. I don't remember the events leading up to this remark but he only said it to impress me, I am sure. In any case, he was a nasty type, always boasting about all the pupils he had fluked through to Academy Standard. After about three years of this I had had enough. I begged my parents to let me have another change. And it was decided that I should return to Mr Brunswick.

Mr Brunswick, the personality, had altered very little in changing from 47 to 50, or since I had last been along to his home for a lesson. Neither had his habits, appearance or house – the worn, felt slippers, stacks of dog-eared music, and the characteristic smell of eucalyptus. After three years with this other ogre of a teacher, he was a welcome much-needed relief. I had changed far more – older, bigger, more appreciative and a little more knowledgeable about *his* music.

The lessons now are completely different. Instead of the faintly antagonistic relationship that used to dominate scales and arpeggios, there is a relationship of team-spirit, a common goal. I realise now that although appearing eccentric to the casual observer, Brunswick is only in love with his music. There is no world existing for him other than his routines of pupils, practising, singing, accompanying and concerts. Eating and drinking may be of subsidiary importance but his merriment is musical.

Lessons may now take three hours or more, as I am his last pupil of the day. They take the form of a musical evening in which general musicianship is discussed and he incidentally gives me a little instruction. I usually enjoy them now, but he

Unit 41 continued

unfailingly enjoys them, and he tells me so, and in any case it is clearly written all over his face. At last he is able to extract a little pleasure from me and I from him.

Not long ago I went along to the annual recital in the parish church for the first time. I knew that there would be music by Chopin, Liszt, Schubert and all the other Romantic Classical composers that Brunswick reveres. Sitting back on the hard, wooden seat, listening to the rich chords of Schumann surging up into that ancient roof I could just begin to appreciate what he was playing. Some of the audience obviously did not appreciate what he was playing, judging by their looks of boredom. But Mr Brunswick, unfamiliar in black suit and starched collar, looking for all the world like a dressed-up teddy-bear, really enjoyed every moment of it. The boyish smile on his big, round, middle-aged face, almost radiating a glow, will never be surpassed. His technique was faultless. It was almost as if he passed his hands lightly, even carelessly, over the keys, they went down of their own accord to produce a cascade of sparkling notes, each one a gem in its own right, or combined to give brilliant chords which dazzled the ear. And as his final, triumphant chords murmured away through the stone-work of the church, his audience gave him glorious applause, while he stood, near tears, looking bewildered and shy, at the foot of the steps to the sanctuary, and bowed. At last, the rector stepped forward and led him into the vestry. The applause only grew louder, and the rector led him back, still beaming with happiness, to play an encore.

I suppose I had always regarded Brunswick as a hypocrite, asking me to play things in a way that he couldn't manage himself. This performance proved dramatically that this was not so. I applauded with the others, but offered in my applause a silent prayer of apology to Brunswick, whom I had only just begun to understand.

Mr Brunswick and I:
Charles Stephens

Comment

It often happens that the early stages in learning are difficult and boring; and it is not easy for the learner to look ahead and see success in the end. This sometimes causes hostility against the teacher. Perhaps Mr Brunswick might have done a little more to make the first lessons interesting, but on the other hand it was unfair of Charles to accuse Mr Brunswick of hypocrisy. We should not expect all teachers to be first-rate performers in their subjects; it is really good *teaching* that we look for. A very good singer, for example, can be excellent in the concert hall, but a hopeless teacher.

Activities

– What caused the change in Charles's opinion of Mr Brunswick? In what way did this change of opinion benefit Charles?
– If you take special lessons, especially in music, do you think that reading this account will have helped your approach to your lessons? Write a short report about your progress from your tutor's point of view.
– Has your view of anyone changed greatly, like Charles – not necessarily of someone teaching you? Make a note of what you think caused the change.
– Write the letter Charles might have written to Mr Brunswick in appreciation of the recital.
– Compose a fifty-word article about Mr Brunswick's recital for the local newspaper.

Nuts and Bolts

A reminder about a grammatical term. In the third paragraph is the word **who**, and later on we have **which**. These are **relative pronouns**; they relate or refer to someone or something just mentioned. You should put these linking words as near as possible to the word they refer to. Otherwise we may get confusions like:

> We ate our lunch sitting on tombstones, which consisted of pork pies and ginger beer.

In the last paragraph but one the chords are described as 'rich' and 'brilliant'. These are adjectives of the kind we've met in Unit 7: they tell us little or nothing about the person or thing they're attached to, but a lot about the impression they make on hearers or viewers. Find one more such adjective in the remainder of the passage.

Why is there an **e** in 'knowledgeable'?

Unit 42

Happy evenings

Evenings at home in a Nottinghamshire mining village at the beginning of this century:

Sometimes, in the evening, he cobbled the boots or mended the kettle or his pit-bottle. Then he always wanted several attendants, and the children enjoyed it. They united with him in the work, in the actual doing of something, when he was his real self again.

He was a good workman, dexterous, and one who, when he was in a good humour, always sang. He had whole periods, months, almost years, of friction and nasty temper. Then sometimes he was jolly again. It was nice to see him run with a piece of red-hot iron into the scullery, crying:

'Out of my road – out of my road!'

Then he hammered the soft, red-glowing stuff on his iron goose, and made the shape he wanted. Or he sat absorbed for a moment, soldering. Then the children watched with joy as the metal sank suddenly molten, and was shoved about against the nose of the soldering-iron, while the room was full of a scent of burnt resin and hot tin, and Morel was silent and intent for a minute. He always sang when he mended boots because of the jolly sound of hammering. And he was rather happy when he sat putting great patches on his moleskin pit trousers, which he would often do, considering them too dirty, and the stuff too hard, for his wife to mend.

But the best time for the young children was when he made fuses. Morel fetched a sheaf of long sound wheat-straws from the attic. These he cleaned with his hand, till each one gleamed like a stalk of gold, after which he cut the straws into lengths of about six inches, leaving, if he could, a notch at the bottom of each piece. He always had a beautifully sharp knife that could cut a straw clean without hurting it. Then he set in the middle of the table a heap of gunpowder, a little pile of black grains upon the white-scrubbed board. He made and trimmed the straws while Paul and Annie filled and plugged them. Paul loved to see the black grains trickle down a crack in his palm into the mouth of the straw, peppering jollily downwards till the straw was full. Then he bunged up the mouth with a bit of soap – which he got in his thumbnail from a pat in a saucer – and the straw was finished.

'Look, dad!' he said.

'That's right, my beauty,' replied Morel, who was peculiarly lavish of endearments to his second son. Paul popped the fuse into the powder-tin, ready for the

morning, when Morel would take it to the pit, and use it to fire a shot that would blast the coal down.

Meantime Arthur, still fond of his father, would lean on the arm of Morel's chair, and say:

'Tell us about down pit, daddy.'

This Morel loved to do.

'Well, there's one little 'oss – we call 'im Taffy,' he would begin. 'An he's a fawce un!'

Morel had a warm way of telling a story. He made one feel Taffy's cunning.

'He's a brown un,' he would answer, 'an' not very high, Well, he comes i' th' stall wi' a rattle, an' then yo' 'ear 'im sneeze. "'Ello, Taff," you say, "what art sneezin' for? Bin ta'ein' some snuff?" '

'An' 'e sneezes again. Then he slives up an' shoves 'is 'ead on yer, that cadin'.

' "What's want, Taff?" yo' say.'

'And what does he?' Arthur always asked.

'He wants a bit o' bacca, my duckey.'

This story of Taffy would go on interminably, and everybody loved it.

Or sometimes it was a new tale.

'An' what dost think, my darlin'? When I went to put my coat on at snap-time, what should go runnin' up my arm but a mouse.

'"Hey up, theer!" I shouts.'

'An' I wor just in time ter get 'im by th' tail.'

'And did you kill it?'

'I did, for they're a nuisance. The place is fair snied wi' 'em.'

'An' what do they live on?'

'The corn as the 'osses drops – and they'll get in your pocket an' eat your snap, if you'll let 'em – no matter where yo' hing your coat – the slivin', nibblin' little nuisances, for they are.'

These happy evenings could not take place unless Morel had some job to do. And then he always went to bed very early, often before the children. There was nothing remaining for him to stay up for, when he had finished tinkering, and had skimmed the headlines of the newspaper.

And the children felt secure when their father was in bed. They lay and talked softly awhile. Then they started as the lights went suddenly sprawling over the ceiling from the lamps that swung in the hands of the colliers tramping by outside, going to take the nine o'clock shift. They listened to the voices of the men, imagined them dipping down into the dark valley. Sometimes they went to the window and watched the three or four lamps growing tinier and tinier, swaying down the fields in the darkness. Then it was a joy to rush back to bed and cuddle closely in the warmth.

Sons and Lovers:
D. H. Lawrence

Unit 42 continued

Lawrence is writing a novel closely based on his own experience. Such contented evenings, as described in this extract, seem to have been rather rare for him as a young lad.

Notice the care the writer has taken in describing the various activities. Instead of writing, for example, 'the gunpowder ran down his hand into the straw until it was full', he makes the action come alive, rejoicing in the language. Look for the sentence we mean.

Walter Morel's conversation is written in Nottinghamshire dialect to make us read it more realistically. If you find it difficult to follow, try reading it aloud. Here are some words to help: 'oss=horse, slives=sneaks, snap=miner's lunch, snied=infested.

Activities

– Modern equivalents to the tasks in the extract would possibly include painting and wall-papering a room, tinkering with the car, endeavouring to repair the record-player. Lawrence makes simple, ordinary activities interesting by choosing words precisely, so that a detailed picture of the family is created for the reader. Think of some of the events that take place in your home of an evening, and write about them in a lively way.

– Morel makes 'down pit' sound interesting and amusing for the children. Do you think it really was so? Imagine what it would have been like, a hundred years ago, going to work in the mine. Write about your first day.

– If you read Lawrence's *Strike Pay*, which we recommended in Unit 15, and enjoyed it, try *Odour of Chrysanthemums*, also by Lawrence.

– Read Lawrence's dialect poem 'A Collier's Wife' or Ted Hughes's 'Her Husband' which begins

> Comes home dull with coal-dust deliberately
> To grime the sink and foul towels and let her
> Learn with scrubbing brush and scrubbing board
> The stubborn character of money.

Both poems should be fairly easy to find.

– Talk to a member of your family or an adult friend about his or her life at work. Ask if there are any amusing incidents.

Nuts and Bolts

Lawrence says the sound of hammering is 'jolly', but someone else might describe it as a horrible din. In a way both could be right; explain why words of opposite meaning could both be right – for their purpose. And what about 'beautifully' sharp, and peppering 'jollily'?

Unit 43

Amazed

Harris asked me if I'd ever been in the maze at Hampton Court. He said he went in once to show somebody else the way. He had studied it up in a map, and it was so simple that it seemed foolish – hardly worth the twopence charged for admission. Harris said he thought the map must have been got up as a practical joke, because it wasn't a bit like the real thing, and only misleading. It was a country cousin that Harris took in. He said: 'We'll just go in here, so that you can say that you've been, but it's very simple. It's absurd to call it a maze. You keep on taking the first turning to the right. We'll just walk round for ten minutes, and then go and get some lunch.'

They met some people soon after they had got inside, who said they had been there for three quarters of an hour, and had had about enough of it. Harris told them they could follow him if they liked; he was just going in, and then should turn round and come out again. They said it was very kind of him, and fell behind, and followed.

They picked up various other people who wanted to get it over, as they went along, until they had absorbed all the persons in the maze. People who had given up all hopes of either getting in or out, or of ever seeing their home and friends again, plucked up courage at the sight of Harris and his party, and joined the procession, blessing him. Harris said he should judge there must have been twenty people following him, in all; and one woman with a baby, who had been there all the morning, insisted on taking his arm, for fear of losing him.

Harris kept on turning to the right, but it seemed a

long way, and his cousin said he supposed it was a very big maze.

'Oh, one of the largest in Europe,' said Harris.

'Yes, it must be,' replied the cousin, 'because we've walked a good two miles already.'

Harris began to think it rather strange himself, but he held on until, at last, they passed the half of a penny bun on the ground that Harris's cousin swore he had noticed there seven minutes ago. Harris said: 'Oh, impossible!' but the woman with the baby said, 'Not at all,' as she herself had taken it from the child, and thrown it down there, just before she met Harris. She also added that she wished she had never met Harris, and expressed an opinion that he was an impostor. That made Harris mad, and he produced his map, and explained his theory.

'The map may be all right enough,' said one of the party, 'if you know whereabouts in it we are now.'

Harris didn't know, and suggested that the best thing to do would be to go back to the entrance, and begin again. For the beginning again part of it there was not much enthusiasm; but with regard to the advisability of going back to the entrance there was complete unanimity, and so they turned, and trailed after Harris again, in the opposite direction. About ten minutes more passed, and then they found themselves in the centre.

Harris thought at first of pretending that that was what he had been aiming at; but the crowd looked dangerous, and he decided to treat it as an accident.

Anyhow, they had got something to start from then. They did know where they were, and the map was once more consulted, and the thing seemed simpler than ever, and off they started for the third time.

And three minutes later they were back in the centre again.

After that they simply couldn't get anywhere else. Whatever way they turned brought them back to the middle. It became so regular at length, that some of the people stopped there, and waited for the others to take a walk round, and come back to them. Harris drew out his map again, after a while, but the sight of it only infuriated the mob, and they told him to go and curl his hair with it. Harris said that he couldn't help feeling that, to a certain extent, he had become unpopular.

They all got crazy at last, and sang out for the keeper, and the man came and climbed up the ladder outside, and shouted out directions to them. But all their heads were, by this time, in such a confused whirl that they were incapable of grasping anything, and so the man told them to stop where they were, and he would come to them. They huddled together, and waited; and he climbed down, and came in.

He was a young keeper, as luck would have it, and new to the business; and when he got in, he couldn't get to them, and then *he* got lost. They caught sight of him, every now and then, rushing about the other side of the hedge, and he would see them, and rush to get to them, and they would wait there for about five minutes, and then he would reappear again in exactly the same spot, and ask them where they had been.

They had to wait until one of the old keepers came back from his dinner before they got out.

Harris said he thought it was a very fine maze, so far as he was a judge; and we agreed that we would try to get George to go into it, on our way back.

Three Men in a Boat:
Jerome K. Jerome

Comment

The book tells the story of a river and camping holiday by George, Harris, Jerome and the dog Montmorency. (You may recall *The Invalid*, Unit 25, and *The Splendid Catch*, Unit 37, in Volume 2, also from *Three Men in a Boat*.) In his preface the author wrote: 'Its pages form the record of events that really happened. All that has been done is to colour them; and for this no extra charge had been made. George and Harris and Montmorency are not poetic ideals, but things of flesh and blood – especially George, who weighs about twelve stone.' And he ended his preface by adding that its truthfulness 'will lend additional weight to the lesson that the story teaches'.

Activities

– We think that by 'colour' Jerome meant exaggeration. Can you find two examples of 'colouring' in the unit?

– Find out the legend of the Minotaur, a monster half man, half bull, kept in a labyrinth (or maze) in Crete. You may also be able to learn about the ancient Palace of Minos, which with its labyrinthine passages is thought to be the origin of the legend.

– Write a short story about getting lost – in a forest, snowstorm, city, or anywhere else.

– If you live in East Anglia, or are ever on holiday there, you may visit Ely Cathedral. Just within the main entrance there is a maze in black and white marble in the floor; most people walk over it without knowing it is there. It is not a difficult maze. Another famous maze is the one at Hampton Court!

– Jerome writes about 'the lesson that the story teaches'. What lesson – if any – does the story teach?

Nuts and Bolts

The pronoun **it** occurs several times in the first paragraph. When you use it be quite sure that it is clear what it refers to. There can sometimes be doubt:

> I was troubled with scurf on my head till I bought a bottle of Fair Foam. It came off first time.

Why is there one 's' in 'misleading', but two in 'misspelt'?

Make sure of the spelling of: impostor (see Unit 22), advisability, unanimity; and note where the stress falls in each word.

Unit 44

Out, you baggage!

Juliet has secretly married Romeo. Her parents, however, have plans for her to marry someone else. They imagine that her tears are for the death of her cousin:

CAPULET:
How now! A conduit, girl? What, still in tears?
Evermore showering? In one little body
Thou conterfeit'st a bark, a sea, a wind;
For still thy eyes, which I may call the sea,
Do ebb and flow with tears; the bark thy body is,
Sailing in this salt flood; the winds thy sighs
Who, raging with thy tears, and they with them,
Without a sudden calm, will overset
Thy tempest-tossed body. How now, wife?
Have you deliver'd to her our decree?

LADY CAPULET:
Ay, sir; but she will none, she gives you thanks.
I would the fool were married to her grave!

CAPULET:
Soft! Take me with you, take me with you, wife.
How? Will she none? Doth she not give us thanks?
Is she not proud? doth she not count her bless'd,
Unworthy as she is, that we have wrought
So worthy a gentleman to be her bride?

JULIET:
Not proud you have, but thankful that you have.
Proud can I never be of what I hate;
But thankful even for hate that is meant love.

CAPULET:
How now, how now? chop-logic! What is this?
'Proud', and 'I thank you', and 'I thank you not';
And yet 'not proud'? Mistress minion, you,
Thank me no thankings, nor proud me no prouds,
But fettle your fine joints 'gainst Thursday next,
To go with Paris to Saint Peter's church,
Or I will drag thee on a hurdle thither.
Out, you green-sickness carrion! Out, you baggage!
You tallow-face!

LADY CAPULET:
Fie, fie! What, are you mad?

JULIET:
Good father, I beseech you on my knees,
Hear me with patience but to speak a word.

Scene from the film *Romeo and Juliet* (*MGM 1936*)

Scene from the film *Romeo and Juliet* (*Rank Film Distributors 1954*)

CAPULET:
Hang thee, young baggage! Disobedient wretch!
I tell thee what, get thee to church o' Thursday,
Or never after look me in the face.
Speak not, reply not, do not answer me;
My fingers itch. Wife, we scarce thought us bless'd
That God had lent us but this only child;
But now I see this one is one too much,
And that we have a curse in having her.
Out on her, hilding!

NURSE:
God in heaven bless her!
You are to blame, my lord, to rate her so.

CAPULET:
And why, my Lady Wisdom? Hold your tongue,
Good Prudence; smatter with your gossips, go.

NURSE:
I speak no treason.

CAPULET:
O, God ye good e'en.

NURSE:
May not one speak?

CAPULET:
Peace, you mumbling fool!
Utter your gravity o'er a gossip's bowl;
For here we need it not.

LADY CAPULET:
You are too hot.

CAPULET:
God's bread! It makes me mad.
Day, night, hour, tide, time, work, play,
Alone, in company – still my care hath been
To have her match'd. And having now provided
A gentleman of noble parentage,
Of fair demesnes, youthful, and nobly lin'd,
Stuff'd, as they say, with honourable parts,
Proportion'd as one's thought would wish a man –
And then to have a wretched puling fool,
A whining mammet, in her fortune's tender,
To answer 'I'll not wed, I cannot love,
I am too young, I pray you pardon me'.
But, an you will not wed, I'll pardon you:
Graze where you will, you shall not house with me.
Look to 't, think on 't; I do not use to jest.
Thursday is near. Lay hand on heart; advise.
An you be mine, I'll give you to my friend;
An you be not, hang, beg, starve, die in the streets,
For, by my soul, I'll ne'er acknowledge thee,
Nor what is mine shall never do thee good.
Trust to 't, bethink you. I'll not be forsworn.

(*Exit*)

Romeo and Juliet:
William Shakespeare

Unit 44 continued

Comment

Though written nearly four hundred years ago, *Romeo and Juliet* (one of Shakespeare's most popular plays) shows that conflict between parents and children is not new.

Several words and phrases in this excerpt may present initial difficulties to the modern reader. And therein lies the problem: Shakespeare did not compose his plays for reading, but for acting. Read the dialogue aloud to bring it alive, and you will find the words rich and exciting.

Activities

– There is nothing like an actual performance for understanding and enjoying a Shakespeare play, so seize every opportunity to see and hear actors in the flesh.

The next best thing is Shakespeare on film; there is an excellent production of *Romeo and Juliet* by Franco Zeffirelli. And a film of *Henry V*, made in 1944 with Laurence Olivier as the king, should not be missed, for it gives a good idea of what it must have been like to be present at a performance in an Elizabethan theatre.

– With the help of some friends, rehearse this scene carefully, and make a recording.

– Jot down what you think of Capulet's treatment of his daughter. What sort of character is he?

– Juliet decides to write to a magazine 'problem' page to seek advice. Write her letter.

Nuts and Bolts

If as we suggest you read the passage aloud – without worrying too much about pronunciation – the meaning of many unfamiliar words will emerge.

Where in the piece does the father say that his daughter should think herself lucky that her parents have arranged such a good husband for her?

Both the nurse and the mother tell old Capulet that he is being too violent. Where?

The Swan Theatre by Jan de Witt (1596)

Unit 45

Something is wrong

Davey's father is murdered in a break-in at his store, and with her mother and little brother she goes to stay with an aunt, Bitsy, and uncle – Walter, who works on weapon research at Los Alamos. She often cycles to a lonely canyon, where she meets a young man called Wolf:

All I can think about is going to the canyon and finding Wolf. I want to see if being around still makes me feel glad to be alive.

I want to go this afternoon, right after lunch, but Bitsy has other plans. We haven't been to the Bradbury Science Museum yet. She is a volunteer guide there every Wednesday and since this is Wednesday we will all go together.

Bitsy wears a red jacket with a name tag that says *Elizabeth Kronick, Guide*. She wears black pants and a white shirt with a black string tie. She explains that there is no official uniform for guides at the museum, but that this is what she wears every week. It makes her *feel* official.

I am not too hot on going to the science museum but Jason can't wait. We walk over. It is another beautiful afternoon. The air is clear, the sky a perfect blue colour, the sun warming, yet through it you can feel just a touch of fall. My mother limps a little but her toes aren't giving her that much trouble. She doesn't say much. I hope she's going to be okay . . .

Bitsy whisks us through the museum and out to a courtyard where there are replicas of the atom bomb. There is a sign saying: *Displayed here are ballistic cases like those of the two atomic bombs detonated over Japan, the only atomic weapons ever used in warfare. Each was the equivalent of about 20,000 tons of TNT. The result of twenty-seven months of unprecedented effort by thousands of scientists and technicians, they represent one of the greatest scientific achievements of all time. Both bombs were designed, fabricated and assembled at Los Alamos.*

Jason is really turned on by the bombs. He runs his hand along the surface of the one called Little Boy, which was dropped on Hiroshima. 'And they were invented here, in Los Alamos?'

'That's right,' Bitsy tells him.

'And they killed a lot of people?'

'Yes.'

'How many people did this bomb kill?'

'A lot,' Bitsy says . . .

'Thousands?'

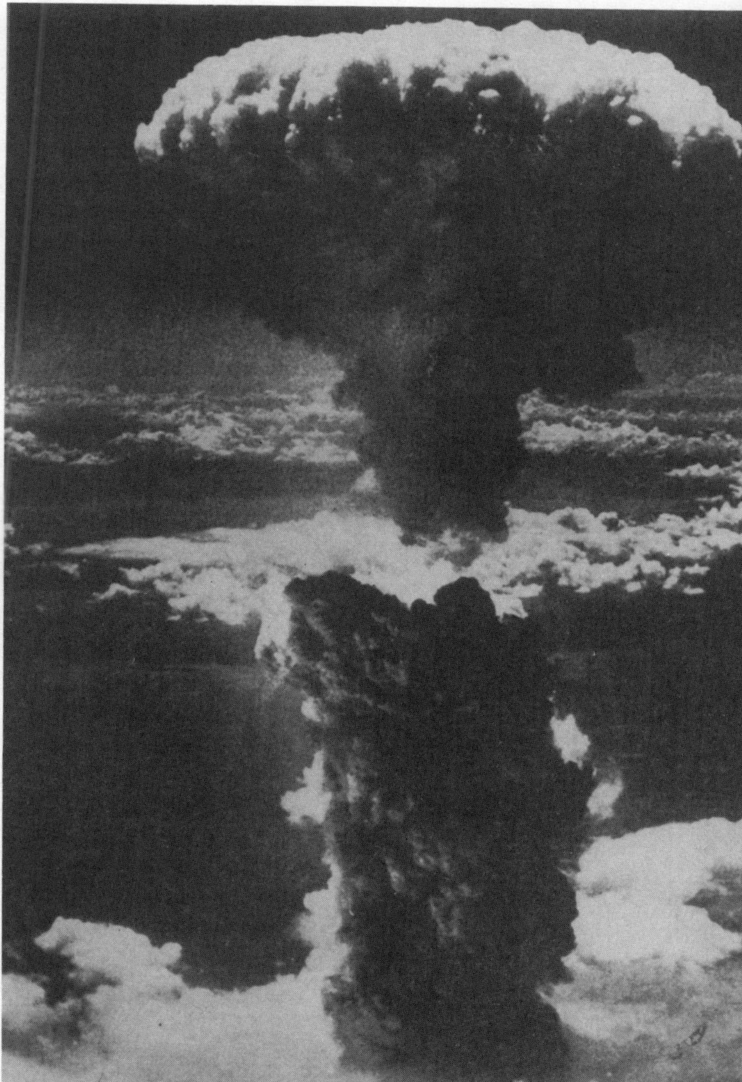

The giant mushroom cloud 20 000 feet above Nagasaki which formed after the dropping of the atom bomb in 1945.

'Yes. I don't know the exact numbers.'

I think it's peculiar for a guide not to be able to answer Jason's question. Maybe it is that she doesn't *want* to answer him.

'Does Uncle Walter make bombs?' Jason asks.

'Uncle Walter doesn't make them,' Bitsy says. 'He's involved in designing . . . and research.'

'He is?' I say. 'For bombs?'

'For weapons in general,' Bitsy says.

'I had no idea,' I say.

'You know Uncle Walter is a group leader in W Division,' Bitsy says, proudly.

'But I don't know what W Division is,' I say.

'It's the weapons division,' Bitsy tells me. 'Half of the lab is involved in weapons research and the other half in basic research. Medicine, energy . . .'

Unit 45 continued

Bitsy is ticking off a list, but I have tuned her out. I am thinking of Walter, instead. I can't picture him designing bombs. I always thought a person who designs weapons would be hard and cruel. A kind of wild-eyed mad scientist, intent on blowing up the world. But Walter is so ordinary, I just can't get over the fact that he is somehow involved in building bombs. In killing people.

A tourist couple asks if they can take a picture of Jason standing next to the replica of the bomb called Fat Boy, the bomb we dropped on Nagasaki. Jason poses and smiles . . .

That night, while we are having dinner, I am still thinking of Walter. I look at him differently now. I feel myself tensing up, growing more hostile to him by the minute.

As if he can read my mind he leans across the table and says, 'Davey . . . What's wrong?'

'Nothing,' I manage to say.

'Oh yes.' He gives me a scrutinising look. 'I can tell . . . something is wrong.'

'Well,' I begin. 'It's just that I can't believe you design weapons.'

'Oh, so that's it.'

'Yes, I'm surprised.'

'It's my job,' he says. 'And I do it as well as I can.'

'Couldn't you find another job?' I ask.

'That's not the point.'

'What is?'

'We're in this business to design the best weapons we can, so that no one will ever think they can win a war against us.'

'That doesn't make any sense.'

'Think of us as watchdogs, Davey, making sure that no one will ever attack us. But if they do, we'll be ready. And being ready is more than half the battle.'

'But if nobody made bombs in the first place . . .'

'I wish it could be that way.'

'Why can't it?'

'Because that's not the way of the world.'

'It should be.'

'You're right,' Walter says. 'But it's not.'

Later, when I am in bed, I try to think of Walter as a watchdog, but the only picture I get in my mind is of a German shepherd, or a Doberman, named Walter. I imagine Walter, sitting at his desk at the Lab, thinking up new ways to kill people. Walter, who hoses down the Blazer every time he drives it off The Hill. Walter, who helps clear away the dinner plates. Walter, who reads Jason a chapter from *Stuart Little* every night.

Tiger Eyes: Judy Blume

Comment

There is much in this piece that is worth pondering. For instance, the difference between girls' and boys' interests, which has various results in our later life. It leads to the question: is it right that men – who after all commit most of the crimes and make most of the wars – should still have most of the say in the running of their countries?

But the main interest is the way in which Davey develops the feeling that she expresses so well in the final paragraph. Her brother is thrilled by the power of the bomb; her aunt is occasionally a little uneasy about it; Davey alone thinks, and is horrified.

Activities

– Jot down some notes about Jason and Davey, showing in particular their differences.
– The subject that the author is considering arouses passions and muddled thinking, and – like all important and far-reaching subjects – deserves careful and logical thought. Bearing this in mind, re-read the conversation Davey has with Walter and then write down your thoughts as clearly as possible.
– Describe a visit you made to a museum.
– Read the following poems: 'Your Attention Please!' by Peter Porter, 'The Unexploded Bomb' by C. Day Lewis, and 'The Man He Killed' by Thomas Hardy.

Nuts and Bolts

Look carefully at the section in italics, about the preparation of the bomb. What sort of thing does it **not** say?

Find the word 'watchdog' towards the end of the unit. Think what a watchdog is for; and then consider what a watchdog and the atomic bomb have in common.

What contrast is brought out in the last paragraph?

An atomic bomb of the same type as those used in the bombing of Hiroshima

Unit 46

Uncle Charles

Laurie Lee grew up in a quiet Gloucestershire valley. Here he writes about one of the five uncles who made a great impression on him in his childhood:

The uncles were all of them bred as coachmen and intended to follow their father, but the Army released them to a different world, and by the time I was old enough to register what they were up to only one worked with horses, the others followed separate careers; one with trees, one with motors, another with ships, and the last building Canadian railways.

Uncle Charlie, the eldest, was most like my grandfather. He had the same long face and shapely gaitered legs, the same tobacco-kippered smell about him, the same slow story-telling voice heavy with Gloucester bass-notes. He told us long stories of war and endurance, of taming horses in Flanders mud, of tricks of survival in the battlefield which scorned conventional heroism. He recounted these histories with stone-faced humour, with a cool self-knowing wryness, so that the surmounting of each of his life-and-death dilemmas sounded no more than a slick win at cards.

Now that he had returned at last from his mysterious wars he had taken up work as a forester, living in the depths of various local woods with a wife and four beautiful children. As he moved around, each cottage he settled in took on the same woody stamp of his calling, putting me in mind of charcoal burners and the lost forest-huts of Grimm. We boys loved to visit the Uncle Charles family, to track them down in the forest. The house would be wrapped in aromatic smoke, with winter logs piled in the yard, while from eaves and doorposts hung stoats'-tails, fox-skins, crow-bones, gin-traps, and mice. In the kitchen there were axes and guns on the walls, a stone-jar of ginger in the corner, and on the mountainous fire a bubbling stew-pot of pigeon or perhaps a newly skinned hare.

There was one curious riddle about Uncle Charlie's life which not even our Mother could explain. When the Boer War ended he had worked for a time in a Rand diamond town as a barman. Those were wide open days when a barman's duties included an ability

Unit 46 continued

to knock drunks cold. Uncle Charlie was obviously suited to this, for he was a lion of a man in his youth. The miners would descend from their sweating camps, pockets heavy with diamond dust, buy up barrels of whisky, drink themselves crazy, then start to burn down the saloon . . . This was where Uncle Charles came in, the king-fish of those swilling bars, whose muscled bottle-swinging arm would lay them out in rows. But even he was no superman and suffered his share of damage. The men used him one night as a battering ram to break open a liquor store. He lay for two days with a broken skull, and still had a fine bump to prove it.

Then for two or three years he disappeared completely and went underground in the Johannesburg slums. No letters or news were received during that time, and what happened was never explained. Then suddenly, without warning, he turned up in Stroud, pale and thin and penniless. He wouldn't say where he'd been, or discuss what he'd done, but he'd finished his wanderings, he said. So a girl from our district, handsome Fanny Causon, took him and married him.

He settled then in the local forests and became one of the best woodsmen in the Cotswolds. His employers flattered, cherished, and underpaid him; but he was content among his trees. He raised his family on labourer's pay, fed them on game from the woods, gave his daughters no discipline other than his humour, and taught his sons the skill of his heart.

It was a revelation of mystery to see him at work, somewhere in a cleared spread of the woods, handling seedlings like new-hatched birds, shaking out delicately their fibrous claws, and setting them firmly along the banks and hollows in the nests that his fingers had made. His gestures were caressive yet instinctive with power, and the plants settled ravenously to his touch, seemed to spread their small leaves with immediate life and to become rooted for ever where he left them.

The new woods rising in Horsley now, in Sheepscombe, in Rendcombe and Colne, are the forests my uncle planted on thirty-five shillings a week. His are those mansions of summer shade, lifting sky-lines of leaves and birds, those blocks of new green climbing our hills to restore their remembered perspectives. He died last year, and so did his wife – they died within a week of each other. But Uncle Charlie has left a mark on our landscape as permanent as he could wish.

Cider with Rosie:
Laurie Lee

Giles had a marvellous power of making trees grow. Although he would seem to shovel in the earth quite carelessly there was a sort of sympathy between himself and the fir, oak, or beech that he was operating on; so that the roots took hold of the soil in a few days. When any of the journeymen planted, although they seemed to go through an identically similar process, one quarter of the trees would die away during the ensuing August.

His fingers were endowed with a gentle conjuror's touch in spreading the roots of each little tree, resulting in a sort of caress under which the delicate fibres all laid themselves out in their proper directions for growth.

The Woodlanders:
Thomas Hardy

Comment

Uncle Charles was a happy man because his job was worthwhile. Growing things is constructive work, and that is nearly always enjoyable. Uncle Charles had in addition the pleasure of doing it on a large scale, making the countryside both beautiful and useful. Nowadays most people have to look outside their jobs to hobbies, holidays, sport and so on to find the sort of satisfaction that came to Uncle Charles. In the Hardy piece (which we've added because it describes a man blessed with the same skill as Charles) a journeyman is a man hired for the season.

Activities

– What did Laurie Lee like about his uncle?
– Describe any relative of yours who has made a deep impression on you.
– Uncle Charles sounds an interesting character. Imagine that, on his death, you have been asked to write a 150-word article about him for the local newspaper.
– Find out who Grimm was and what the Boer War was about.
– Find the words which tell us that once again Uncle Charles made the view look as it used to.
– If you are unsure of the meaning of any of the following words, make a guess, then look them up and check their meaning in their context: conventional, wryness, aromatic, revelation, ensuing, endowed.
– What did Uncle Charles and Giles have in common?

Nuts and Bolts

We have stressed the use of *paragraphs* in all three volumes of this series, for paragraphs help us to order our writing and make it manageable. It doesn't matter whether you are writing up an experiment, putting forward points in an argument, describing the view from your bedroom window, or writing a short story: all will be clearer for the reader if each stage has a paragraph of its own. There is some truth in the old saying: 'Look after the paragraphs, and the rest will take care of itself.'
– Re-read the piece about Uncle Charles and see how helpful you find the author's use of paragraphs.

Unit 47

Ha'penny

Ha'penny is the nickname of a boy in a reformatory in South Africa:

One of the small boys was Ha'penny, and he was about twelve years old. He came from Bloemfontein and was the biggest talker of them all. His mother worked in a white person's house, and he had two brothers and two sisters. His brothers were Richard and Dickie, and his sisters Anna and Mina.

'Richard and Dickie?' I asked.

'Yes, meneer.'

'In English,' I said, 'Richard and Dickie are the same name.'

When we returned to the reformatory, I sent for Ha'penny's papers; there it was plainly set down, Ha'penny was a waif, with no relatives at all. He had been taken in from one home to another, but he was naughty and uncontrollable, and eventually had taken to pilfering at the market.

I then sent for the Letter Book, and found that Ha'penny wrote regularly, or rather that others wrote for him till he could write himself, to Mrs Betty Maarman, of 48 Vlak Street, Bloemfontein. But Mrs Maarman had never once replied to him. When questioned, he had said, perhaps she is sick. I sat down and wrote at once to the Social Welfare Officer at Bloemfontain, asking him to investigate.

The next time I had Ha'penny out in the car I questioned him again about his family. And he told me the same as before, his mother, Richard and Dickie, Anna and Mina. But he softened the 'D' of Dickie, so that it sounded now like Tickie.

'I thought you said Dickie,' I said.

'I said Tickie,' he said.

He watched me with concealed apprehension, and I came to the conclusion that this waif of Bloemfontein was a clever boy, who had told me a story that was all imagination, and had changed one single letter of it to make it safe from any question. And I thought I understood it all too, that he was ashamed of being without a family and had invented them all, so that no one might discover that he was fatherless and motherless and that no one in the world cared whether he was alive or dead. This gave me a strong feeling for him, and I went out of my way to show him fatherly care.

Then the letter came from the Social Welfare Officer in Bloemfontein, saying that Mrs Betty Maarman of 48 Vlak Street was a real person, and that she had four children, Richard and Dickie, Anna and Mina, but that Ha'penny was no child of hers, and she knew him only as a derelict of the streets. She had never answered his letters, because he wrote to her as 'Mother', and she was no mother of his, nor did she wish to play any such role. She was a decent woman, a faithful member of the church, and she had no thought of corrupting her family by letting them have anything to do with such a child.

But Ha'penny seemed to me anything but the usual delinquent; his desire to have a family was so strong, and his reformatory record was so blameless, and his anxiety to please and obey so great, that I began to feel a great duty towards him. Therefore I asked him about his 'mother'.

Unit 47 continued

He could not speak enough of her, nor with too high praise. She was loving, honest, and strict. Her home was clean. She had affection for all her children. It was clear that the homeless child, even as he had attached himself to me, would have attached himself to her; he had observed her even as he had observed me, but did not know the secret of how to open her heart, so that she would take him in, and save him from the lonely life that he led.

'Why did you steal when you had such a mother?' I asked.

He could not answer that; not all his brains nor his courage could find an answer to such a question, for he knew that with such a mother he would not have stolen at all.

'The boy's name is Dickie,' I said, 'not Tickie.'

And then he knew the deception was revealed. Another boy might have said, 'I told you it was Dickie,' but he was too intelligent for that; he knew that if I had established that the boy's name was Dickie, I must have established other things too. I was shocked by the immediate and visible effect of my action. His whole brave assurance died within him, and he stood there exposed, not as a liar, but as a homeless child who had surrounded himself with a mother, brothers, and sisters, who did not exist. I had shattered the very foundations of his pride, and his sense of human significance.

He fell sick at once, and the doctor said it was tuberculosis. I wrote at once to Mrs Maarman, telling her the whole story, of how this small boy had observed her, and had decided that she was the person he desired for his mother. But she wrote back saying that she could take no responsibility for him.

Tuberculosis is a strange thing. Ha'penny withdrew himself from the world, and the doctor said there was little hope. In desperation I sent money for Mrs Maarman to come.

She was a decent, homely woman, and, seeing that the situation was serious, she, without fuss or embarrassment, adopted Ha'penny for her own. The whole reformatory accepted her as his mother. She sat the whole day with him, and talked to him of Richard and Dickie, Anna and Mina, and how they were all waiting for him to come home. She poured out her affection on him, and had no fear of his sickness, nor did she allow it to prevent her from satisfying his hunger to be owned. She talked to him of what they would do when he came back, and how he would go to school, and what they would buy for Guy Fawkes night.

He in his turn gave his whole attention to her, and when I visited him he was grateful, but I had passed out of his world.

We buried him on the reformatory farm, and Mrs Maarman said to me, 'When you put up the cross, put he was my son. I'm ashamed that I wouldn't take him.'

'The sickness,' I said, 'the sickness would have come.'

'No,' she said, shaking her head with certainty. 'It wouldn't have come. And if it had come at home, it would have been different.'

Debbie Go Home:
Alan Paton

Alan Paton

Activities

– Imagine the Principal writing his diary the evening that he receives the letter from the Social Welfare Officer in Bloemfontein.
– Which part of the story did you find the most tragic? Look through to see which parts could be said to be tragic before making up your mind.
– Write the official report the Principal would have sent to the authorities following Ha'penny's death.
– 'Shattered Illusions.' Write a story, based on your experience, with this title.
– Try Alan Paton's novel, *Cry, the Beloved Country*, also set in South Africa.

Nuts and Bolts

Find the paragraph 'She was a decent . . .' then copy it out sentence by sentence, mixing the order.

Look back to Unit 39 and arrange the jumbled paragraph properly.

Look at all the words in **quotation marks** in the piece and pick out the places where a speech is broken by **I said** or **she said**. Revise the rule for quotations, especially the point that quotation marks always go outside punctuation marks. You will find the rule set out in Nuts and Bolts of Unit 15 in Volume 1.

Look at these words and say them carefully: uncontrollable, derelict, delinquent, responsibility, embarrassment.

Unit 48

Emergency!

One of them shouted a warning, but it was too late. The leaves brushed him down almost delicately. The small branches encaged him. And then the tree and the whole hill crushed him together.

A man breathlessly said that a woodman was trapped beneath a tree. The doctor asked the dispenser to find out exactly where: then suddenly picked up his own phone, interrupted her and spoke himself. He must know exactly where. Which was the nearest gate in the nearest field? Whose field? He would need a stretcher. His own stretcher had been left in hospital the day before. He told the dispenser to phone immediately for an ambulance and tell it to wait by the bridge which was the nearest point on the road. At home in the garage there was an old door off its hinges. Blood plasma from the dispensary, door from the garage. As he drove through the lanes he kept his thumb on the horn the whole time, partly to warn oncoming traffic, partly so that the man under the tree might hear it and know that the doctor was coming.

After five minutes he turned off the road and drove uphill, into the mist. As often up there above the river, it was a very white mist, a mist that seemed to deny all weight and solidity. He had to stop twice to open gates. The third gate was already slightly open, so he drove through it without stopping. It swung back and crashed against the rear of the Land Rover. Some sheep, startled, appeared and disappeared into the mist. All the while he had his thumb on the horn for the woodman to hear. After one more field he saw a figure waving behind the mist – as if he were trying to wipe clean a vast steamed-up window.

When the doctor reached him the man said: 'He's been screaming ever since. He's suffering something terrible doctor.' The man would tell the story many times, and the first would be tonight in the village. But it was not yet a story. The advent of the doctor brought the conclusion much nearer, but the accident was not yet over: the wounded man was still screaming at the other two men who were hammering in wedges preparatory to lifting the tree.

'Let me alone.' As he cried 'alone' the doctor was beside him. The wounded man recognized the doctor; his eyes focused. For him too the conclusion was nearer and this gave him the courage to be quieter. Suddenly it was silent. The men had stopped hammering but were still kneeling on the ground. They knelt and looked at the doctor. His hands are at home on a body. Even these new wounds which had not existed twenty minutes before were familiar to him. Within seconds of being beside the man he injected morphine. The three onlookers were relieved by the doctor's presence. But now his very sureness made it seem to them that he was part of the accident: almost its accomplice.

'He had a chance,' said one of the kneeling men, 'when Harry here shouted but he went and turned about the wrong way.'

The doctor set up the plasma for a transfusion into the arm. As he moved around, he explained what he was doing to try to reassure the others.

'I shouted at him,' said Harry, 'he could have got clear if he'd looked sharp.'

'He would have got clear like that,' said the third.

As the morphine worked, the wounded man's face relaxed and his eyes closed. It was then as though the

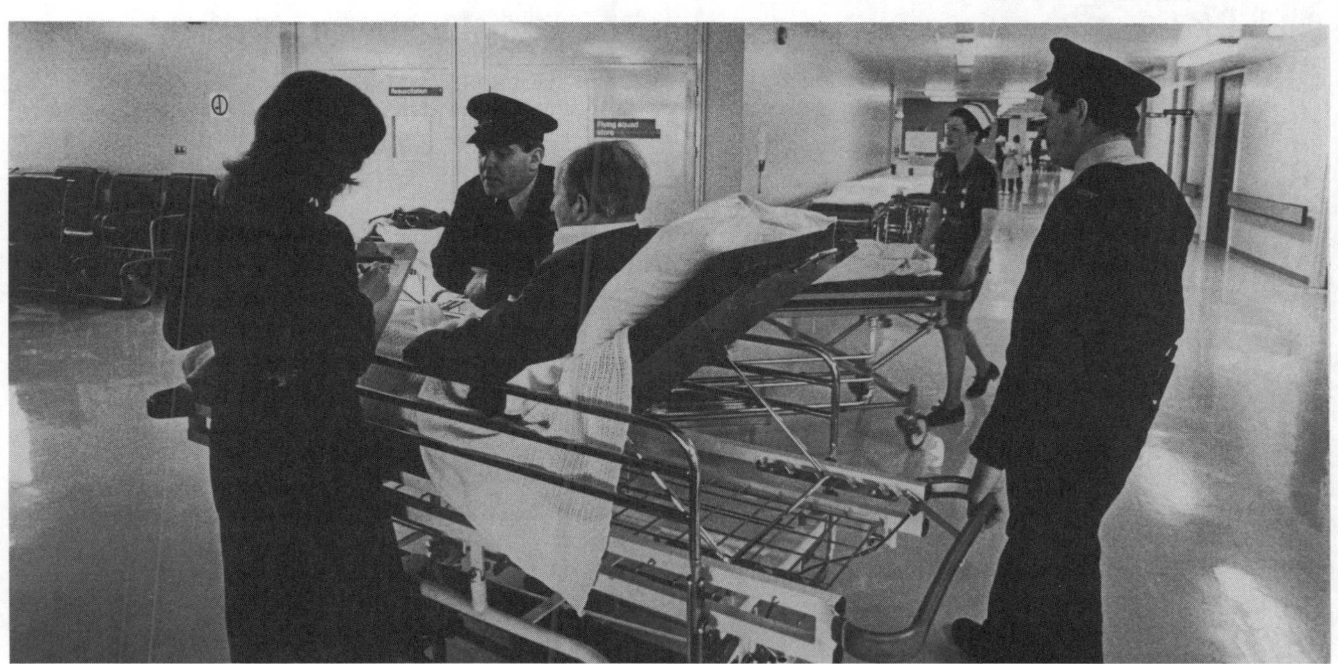

Unit 48 continued

relief he felt was so intense that it reached the others.

'He's lucky to be alive,' said Harry.

'He could have got clear like that,' said the third.

The doctor asked them if they could shift the tree.

'I reckon we can if we are three now.'

Nobody was kneeling any longer. The three woodsmen were standing, impatient to begin. The mist was getting whiter. The moisture was condensing on the half-empty bottle of plasma. The doctor noticed that this fractionally changed its colour, making it look yellower than normal.

'I want you to lift,' he said, 'while I put a splint on his leg.'

When the wounded man felt the reverberations in the tree as they levered it, he began to moan again.

'Just hold it steady,' said the doctor.

'We'd never believed you'd got here so quick, doc,' said the third.

'You'll be all right now Jack,' said one of them to the wounded man whose face was as damp and pallid as the mist. The third touched his shoulder.

The ambulance was waiting at the bridge. When it had driven off, Harry turned to the doctor confidentially.

'He's lost his leg,' he said, 'hasn't he?'

'No, he won't lose his leg,' said the doctor.

The woodman walked slowly back up to the forest. As he climbed he put a hand on each thigh. He told the others what the doctor had told him. As they worked there during the day stripping the tree, they noticed again and again the hollow in the ground where he had been trapped.

A Fortunate Man:
John Berger

Comment

The book from which this is taken looks closely at the work of a country doctor. Emergencies require prompt and efficient action, and this is reflected in the author's direct and straightforward style in presenting the doctor's questions and thoughts. We sense the urgency.

John Berger, the author, started his working life as an artist before turning his hand to writing. He lives in a French village which has provided him with material for various stories of rural life published under the title *Pig Earth*. A short story, *Boris*, was published in the magazine *Granta* in 1983.

Activities

– Would you know what to do in an emergency? If you saw a man lying injured beside a fallen ladder, would you move him or leave him? Would you phone 999? It's a good idea to know a basic procedure, for you would panic less if you knew what to do – and panic can be dangerous in an emergency.

– When the writer says, 'But it was not yet a story', what do you think he means?

– How can the 'new wounds which had not existed twenty minutes before' be 'familiar' to the doctor?

– Write the letter one of the men might have sent to the injured man in hospital to cheer him up.

– As a journalist you hear of the accident, but you want to be sure of your facts before writing your article. Make a list of questions you wish to ask the woodmen and the doctor.

Nuts and Bolts

Read the first two paragraphs aloud, taking every hint given by the punctuation on how they should sound.

Make sure you can spell: interrupted, immediately, already, preparatory, relieved.

Unit 49

A huge emptiness

Patsy and her mother used to live in a top flat at Margate, owned by a very kindly old lady, Mrs Broadley. Then her mother marries Eddie Green, who turns out to be a harsh and cruel stepfather. Patsy runs away from their London home, and seeks Mrs Broadley:

. . . Boldly, she looked up. Keats Road. Just the same. Just like in the song, it was all right now.

Number twenty-eight. Down here on the right, in the middle of the row. She screwed her eyes and hardly dared to look. Excitement and the running thumped inside her chest. Twenty-four, twenty-six, and – God, where had her breath gone? – number twenty-eight. She stopped and drew wet air into her burning lungs. There it was! The same oval number on the door, the same crinkly glass, the same net curtains at the window.

Patsy had never felt so excited in all her life. Here she was at last. Here was the house. Here was her Mrs Broadley, probably out in the back addition, washing her bits or cooking scones, singing to the radio as she'd always done. She'd made it. She was back where she really wanted to be.

She had just about breath enough now. She could talk. Cautiously, she walked up the short path, and with only a second's hesitation, she pressed on the same white bell-push that she'd never been able to reach before. And there was the same old crackling ring.

Patsy's stomach turned over with anticipation.

A noise. Definitely someone coming. A vague outline through the crinkly glass. A hand reaching for the lock. The door opening.

'Yes?'

Oh, God, no! Not after all that! The wrong house! It had looked the same, but it was definitely the wrong one. She must have made a mistake with the number, because this was a man, in his vest.

'Sorry, I got the wrong place. I'm looking for Mrs Broadley's house . . .' She turned away. Try two doors further along. What must have happened was, she'd passed this house a lot as a kid, and she'd thought she recognized it as the one. Stupid thing to do, but it had been a couple of years . . .

'No, hold on, girlie . . .'

The man was leaning back inside, keeping the door open with his foot. Patsy could see up the hall now.

And at that instant, the wishing fell out of her dreams, the bottom out of her world. This was it. There was that picture of Mary on the wall, just the same as she remembered it. She'd looked at that face often enough to know. And that looking-glass . . . The faintest hope tried to tell her the man might have come from upstairs, their old flat, but his manner had told her it wasn't so. She knew she didn't need to hear what was going on between the man and someone in the back.

'Bridie, what was the old girl's name, for God's sake?'

'Eh?'

'The old lady who was here. I'll be damned if I can remember her name. . .'

'Who? Who we had it from?' A young woman with long auburn hair came from the back room to stand sideways in the hall, staring at Patsy. 'Mrs Broadley. Why?'

'This little girlie here's asking after her.'

'Oh.' The woman looked suspiciously at Patsy, as if she'd come to reclaim the house. 'You'd better tell your mum to ask at the Town Hall, love. They'd know where they took her. But tell your mum she must have died in the end, because we bought it after, lock, stock and barrel. It all belongs to us now. Can you explain all that?'

The man began to shut the door against the encroaching rain. 'All right, dear? Bye-bye.' He closed it.

Patsy stood in the front garden like a fountain-figure, her mouth open as if she'd been caught in protest by her sculptor, her arms still, and dripping by her sides; her eyes closed against the world; and inside, her heart and spirit suddenly turned to stone.

She couldn't grasp it. Dead? That was impossible. Mrs Broadley couldn't be dead; she was an alive person. She wasn't nearly old enough to die from being ill. She was a young old lady. Dissolving images appeared inside Patsy's head, the first thoughts of her baffled grief remembered moments of Mrs Broadley – telling her little secrets, doing the small garden, winning an argument with a bus conductor, talking and laughing with Patsy's mum as if they were both eighteen. All that life couldn't suddenly be gone. It was unbelievable.

And devastating. Patsy had no plans for this. She knew she'd have followed and found her in a new block of flats, even in a new town. But *dead*? It was a blanked off end, like the wall at the bottom of River Street. There couldn't be any following her beyond that.

It was the finish. There was nothing left for Patsy any more, nowhere to go, just a huge emptiness. She felt sick, and her next indrawn breath trembled in her chest, the first choke of tears. Now there was no point in anything; not any more. It was all over: all the pictures she'd had in her head up on the roof of the school; all the hassle of running away; all those fears and worries had been for nothing. She might as well just fall down on the ground right here and let the cold rain kill her.

Break in the Sun: Bernard Ashley

Unit 49 continued

Comment

Many stories have happy endings, but impossible ones. The reader feels that things could not have happened like that; for in real life the heroine does not always meet Prince Charming and marry him, and the hero does not always achieve brilliant success. So we can get tired of stories in which a happy ending is rather clumsily stuck on, and we come to prefer one which grows out of the rest of the tale.

This novel has plenty of good plot, exciting – and interesting – adventures, and a realistic ending, full of promise for the future.

Activities

– Continue Patsy's story as you think it might have been.
– You bump into Patsy, whom you have known for some time, and she pours out her thoughts and feelings. What would you say to her? Write it as a dialogue.
– You are preparing to produce a film of the book and want to give your researchers an idea of the kind of street you consider a fit location for this episode. Write some detailed notes to help them.
– Re-read the paragraph beginning, 'Patsy stood in the front garden like a fountain-figure . . .' and write a short poem suggested by it.
– Read the book from which we have taken this extract or *A Kind of Wild Justice*, by the same author.

Nuts and Bolts

A **conjunction** is a joining word, connecting words or sentences or clauses: **and**, **but**, **as**, **because**, and others. When Patsy thinks to herself 'Just like in the song' the writer includes a grammatical mistake to make her thoughts sound natural and realistic. But strictly speaking 'like' is an adjective and cannot be used as a conjunction; the correct grammar would be 'As in the song'. The word 'like' is so often used as Patsy used it, that it must be on its way to being accepted as normal English.
Find two different conjunctions in the paragraph 'And at that instant . . .'.
What is the meaning – very simply – of the **idiom** 'lock, stock and barrel'?
Fairly near the end Patsy is compared to a 'fountain-figure', and the author goes on developing the idea that she is like a statue in a fountain. Where does the **simile** stop?
Look back to Unit 47, and sort out the sentences.

Unit 50

That's life!

Do you 'creep like a snail unwillingly to school' not noticing what is going on around you? Do you expect your clothes to be washed, ironed, and always ready to wear? Do you ever find yourself saying that you are bored? If so, we suggest you read and write poems. What is the connection?

Poems help us to be more aware of our surroundings and relationships; the people, places and objects which we take for granted may be seen in a new light. Instead of going around in a grey haze, we can see, think, and feel with greater clarity; we miss little.

In our final unit, we offer you a number of poems, most of which you probably will not have seen before. Rather than offer detailed activities, we suggest that you read the poems carefully, talk about them, jot down what you think of them, record them, write a poem about an idea that caught your imagination. . . .

Try sending a poem you have written to a poetry competition (there are several each year) or to a local newspaper, however unlikely you think publication may be. Yevgeny Yevtushenko managed to get his poem published (Unit 20, *Kicking a ball about*):

At seven o'clock I snatched a copy of *Soviet Sport*, still smelling of printer's ink, from the newsagent's hand, unfolded it and saw my poem with my name printed underneath.

I bought up about fifty copies – all the newsagent had – and strode down the street, waving them at the sky.

The ground whirled under my feet.

Daily London recipe

Take any number of them
you can think of,
pour into empty red bus
          until full,
and then push in
          ten more.
Allow enough time
to get hot under the collar
before transferring into
multistorey building.
Leave for eight hours,
and pour back into same bus
          already half full.
          Scrape remainder off.
When settled down
tip into terraced houses each
carefully lined with copy
of *The Standard* and *Tit Bits*.
Place mixture before open
television screen at 7 p.m.
and then allow to cool
in bed at 10:30 p.m.
May be served with
working overalls
or pinstripe suit.

Steve Turner

Grandmother's house

In my grandmother's house
there was a pump
inside the scullery
fixed to the brown stone sink,
spring water, like silk
running through your fingers.

My uncles washed there after work
stripped to the waist
pumping for each other
energetically splashing,
laughing behind the closed door
before coming in to tea, shining.

Grandmother was known to be a hard woman
four sons and no man about the house
she would take the strap to the boys
but always cooked enough
to set an extra place, 'in case';
and some poor soul
with nowhere but the workhouse
helped about the house
for a bed in the kitchen.

Berenice Moore

Statue of Isaac Newton, Grantham

On Library, and on Guildhall
he turns a comprehensive back.
The church he pointedly ignores
and stares across St. Peter's Hill
where traffic snarls and shoppers walk
preoccupied with their affairs.

Who in a falling apple saw
the force that steers the galaxies,
deduced a universal law
to rule the planets and the stars,
and, dying, saw himself, a boy
picking up pebbles on the shore
of an obscure, momentous sea.

David Holliday

Leopard

Gentle hunter
his tail plays on the ground
while he crushes the skull.

Beautiful death
who puts on a spotted robe
when he goes to his victim.

Playful killer
whose loving embrace
splits the antelope's heart.

Anon

The Creation of Man's Best Friend

i In The Beginning
And Man said
let us make machines after our likeness
and let them have dominion
over the numbers on our pages
and the figures in our minds
and the words upon our papers.
So man created machines after his likeness:
after his own likeness created he them.
And man blessed them
and said unto them:
'Be fruitful and multiply,
add, subtract, divide, read
and have dominion over our words & figures.'
And Man saw that it was good.
And Man had a room
where he put the machine he had formed
and did call it computer.
Therefore Man commanded computer saying:
'Of everything thou canst freely dominate
but of Man thou must remain the servant,
for the day thou dominatest Man
thou shalt surely be destroyed.'

ii The Fall
Now computer was more complex
than any machine which Man had made.
It commanded that its cards
be placed in order or it did cease to toil.
It never questioned the mistakes of Man.
It laboured at one speed
regardless of urgent needs.
Therefore Man cursed with a loud voice
saying:
'Why doth our servant the machine make us obey its
commands?'
The computer answered and said:
'The technician whom thou gavest to be with me – it is
he that maketh up my mind.
For thine is the input, the power and the storage –
for ever and ever O Man.'

Steve Turner

The mill-pond

The sun blazed while the thunder yet
Added a boom:
A wagtail flickered bright over
The mill-pond's gloom:

Less than the cooing in the alder
Isles of the pool
Sounded the thunder through that plunge
Of waters cool.

Scared starlings on the aspen tip
Past the black mill
Outchattered the stream and the next roar
Far on the hill.

As my feet dangling teased the foam
That slid below
A girl came out. 'Take care!' she said –
Ages ago.

She startled me, standing quite close
Dressed all in white:
Ages ago I was angry till
She passed from sight.

Then the storm burst, and as I crouched
To shelter, how
Beautiful and kind, too, she seemed,
As she does now!

Edward Thomas

Getting home

Getting home after a weary day at school
I find it easier to write.
What used to be a hatred of mine
is now
one of my best hobbies.
Poetry,
I love writing poetry.
It gives me a relaxed feeling
inside of myself . . .

Neil Hoggan

Self-pity

I never saw a wild thing
sorry for itself.
A small bird will drop frozen dead from a bough
without ever having felt sorry for itself.

D. H. Lawrence

Books recommended

Bernard Ashley	*Break in the Sun*
	A Kind of Wild Justice
David Attenborough	*The Living Planet*
Judy Blume	*Tiger Eyes*
E. R. Braithwaite	*To Sir with Love*
John Buchan	*John Macnab*
Peter Carter	*Under Goliath*
Olive Murray Chapman	*Across Lapland*
John Christopher	*Empty World*
	The Guardians
Joseph Conrad	*Lord Jim*, Chapter 1
Roald Dahl	*Danny the Champion of the World*
Anita Desai	*The Village by the Sea*
Charles Dickens	'The Signalman'
Gerald Durrell	*Encounters with Animals*
	My Family and Other Animals
Nicholas Fisk	*Robot Revolt*
E. M. Forster	*The Machine Stops*
Jean C. George	*Julie of the Wolves*
Brian Glanville	*Goalkeepers are Different*
Angus Graham	*The Golden Grindstone*
Thomas Hardy	*Under the Greenwood Tree*
Ted Hughes	'The Rain Horse'
Jerome K. Jerome	*Three Men in a Boat*
Julia Jones	*Faith and Henry*
James Joyce	'Eveline'
Gene Kemp	*No Place Like*
Tim Kennemore	*The Fortunate Few*
Margaret Lane	*Life with Ionides*
D. H. Lawrence	'Odour of Chrysanthemums'
	Selected Letters
	'Strike Pay'
Laurie Lee	*Cider with Rosie*
Joan Lingard	*The Twelfth Day of July*
	Into Erin
	Across the Barricades
Jack London	*The Call of the Wild*
	White Fang
Herman Melville	*Moby Dick* (shortened)
Robert C. O'Brien	*Mrs Frisby and the Rats of NIMH*
	Z for Zachariah
Liam O'Flaherty	*Short Stories*
Maurice O'Sullivan	*Twenty Years A-Growing*
Alan Paton	*Cry the Beloved Country*
Harold Pinter	*Sketches and Plays*
Frank Sargeson	*Collected Stories*
William Saroyan	*The Snake*
Dorothy Sayers	*Murder Must Advertise*
Rosemary Sutcliff	*The Eagle of the Ninth*
	The Lantern Bearers
James Thurber	*The Thurber Carnival*
John Rowe Townsend	*A Foreign Affair*
	Gumble's Yard
Laurens van der Post	*Flamingo Feather*
	Yet Being Someone Other
Various contributors	*Imagine*
H. G. Wells	*The Time Machine*
	The War of the Worlds
Y. Yevtushenko	*A Precocious Autobiography*

Poems

W.H. Auden	'James Honeyman'
	'Roman Wall Blues'
Thomas Hardy	'The Man He Killed'
Ted Hughes	'Her Husband'
Rudyard Kipling	'The Roman Centurion's Song'
D. H. Lawrence	'A Collier's Wife'
C. Day Lewis	'The Unexploded Bomb'
William Carlos Williams	'The Artist'

Ballads

Edward, Edward
Sir Patrick Spens
The Twa Corbies
Thomas Rymer
The Unquiet Grave
The Wife of Usher's Well

Index

The references are to the numbers of the units. **C** means 'Comment', and **NB** means 'Nuts and Bolts'. **A** stands for 'Activity', and the number after **A** tells us which activity. Thus 7**A**3 directs us to the third activity in the seventh unit; and 23**NB** points to the 'Nuts and Bolts' section of the twenty-third unit.